JESUS

AND PRAYER

What the New Testament Teaches Us

To Brad,
with best
wishes,
Dan
7/7/09

JESUS

AND PRAYER

What the New Testament Teaches Us

D A N I E L   J.   H A R R I N G T O N ,   S J

the WORD among us® press

Published by The Word Among Us Press
9639 Doctor Perry Road
Ijamsville, Maryland 21754
www.wordamongus.org

13 12 11 10 09 1 2 3 4 5
ISBN: 978-1-59325-153-6

Cover design by Christopher Tobias

Cover image: El Greco, (1541-1614), *Christ Blessing*.
Casa y Museo del Greco, Toledo, Spain
Photo Credit: Bridgeman-Giraudon/Art Resource, NY

Made and printed in the United States of America.

Library of Congress Cataloging-in-Publication Data

Harrington, Daniel J.
    Jesus and prayer : what the New Testament teaches us / Daniel J.
Harrington.
        p. cm.
    ISBN 978-1-59325-153-6 (alk. paper)
    1. Jesus Christ—Prayers. 2. Jesus Christ—Teachings. 3. Prayer—Biblical
teaching. I. Title.
    BV229.H37 2009
    242'.722--dc22

                                2009015263

IN MEMORY OF

ROBERT E. MANNING, SJ (1937–2008):

A LOVER OF SACRED SCRIPTURE

Recent Books by Daniel J. Harrington, SJ

What Are They Saying About Mark? (2004)

What Are They Saying About the Letter to the Hebrews (2005)

Jesus Ben Sira of Jerusalem: A Biblical Guide to Living Wisely (2005)

How Do Catholics Read the Bible? (2005)

The Letter to the Hebrews (2006)

What Are We Hoping For? New Testament Images (2006)

Jesus: A Historical Portrait (2007)

Why Do We Hope? Images in the Psalms (2008)

Meeting St. Paul Today (2008)

The Synoptic Gospels Set Free: Preaching without Anti-Judaism (2009)

CONTENTS

Introduction

Since ancient times Christians have turned to the New Testament to learn how to pray. Jesus himself teaches us about prayer, especially in his own prayer to the Father. Prayers by the early Christians about Jesus appear throughout the New Testament letters. As twenty-first century Christians, what can we expect to learn from an exploration of these prayers and the teachings on prayer that appear in the New Testament?

The New Testament consists of four gospels, the Acts of the Apostles, thirteen Pauline epistles, Hebrews, the seven Catholic epistles, and the Book of Revelation. While the bulk of these books are either narratives (gospels and Acts) or instructions and exhortations (epistles), many of them include prayers or instructions on prayer at decisive moments. It is my conviction that by focusing on the passages on prayer in the New Testament, we will see more clearly what the sacred writers thought was most important about Jesus. We will also join the earliest Christians in celebrating him as the definitive revealer and revelation of God.

In this book, I will seek to highlight how these passages and prayers are rooted in the Old Testament and the Jewish heritage of early Christianity. I want to use these prayer texts as a way to better understand Jesus and the early Christian writings that we call the New Testament. Finally, my hope is that such an exploration can help Christians today to integrate their own prayer with the basic prayer texts of the Christian tradition.

JESUS AND PRAYER IN CONTEXT

The title of this book is *Jesus and Prayer*. By "Jesus," I mean not only the historical figure who lived and worked in Palestine in the first century, but also—and especially—the risen Christ, who is the main topic of the New Testament. Christians believe he now reigns in glory with his heavenly Father and will come again. As we will see, the gospels contain prayers by Jesus and teachings about prayer that surely come from him. But the New Testament also provides many prayers and hymns *about* Jesus, especially with regard to his incarnation, saving death, resurrection, and exaltation.

By "prayer," I mean simply the raising of the mind and heart to God and its expression in words. In the Bible there are two basic categories of prayers: praises and petitions. The praises include benedictions, thanksgivings, doxologies, and other modes of expression that extol the greatness of God. The petitions are requests that God act on behalf of the one making the prayer, either on the personal level or in a communal context, or both. The two basic forms often appear in the same prayer, and in the various literary forms or prayer scripts there is a great deal of flexibility. In reading and reflecting on these prayers, it is important always to attend to the following elements in any act of communication: the speaker, the addressee, the medium or literary form, the message, and the purpose.

I hope to look at these writings in the context in which they were written. By "context" I mean three things. First, I will examine the historical setting or cultural milieu in which these prayers were composed (the Old Testament, Judaism, the Greco-Roman world). In attending to their context in the ancient world, we need especially to consider their language, literary forms, and theological assumptions. Second, I will look at the literary framework in which they now appear (the New Testament writings). In dealing with their role in the New Testament writings, we need to discern how they fit within those documents and how they contribute rhetorically to the overall theological message of those books. Third, I will address the situation in which these prayers may be read or prayed today (Christianity in the twenty-first century). In trying to make these prayers more intelligible and available for Christians today, we need to show how these ancient prayers can connect us more closely with the essential elements of the Christian narrative, deepen our relationship with God and Christ, and shape our character and our outlook on the world and other people.

The "Fusion of Horizons"

The method by which these prayers and teachings on prayer will be studied in this book is literary, historical, and theological. In analyzing the texts we will examine their literary context, words and images, plot or progress of thought, literary form, and message. There will also be a serious effort to relate these New Testament passages to their Old Testament roots and Jewish context as well as their place in the early Christian movement. As we will see, most of these prayers deliberately reuse words and images from earlier texts. They place passages chiefly from the Old Testament in fresh combinations and contexts in order to create something new, celebrating what God has done in the past, especially through Jesus the Son of God, and what God will do in the future to bring about the fullness of God's kingdom. This technique is often called the "anthological style" and is very common in Jewish writings of the Second Temple period (537 B.C. to A.D. 70). The texts we will study are most obviously religious texts that claim to speak about God and the ways of God with humankind. And so we will also be concerned with the problems that they presume, with the theological themes that they develop, and with how we in the twenty-first century might best make these prayers our own.

Nevertheless, in the Catholic tradition, the work of biblical interpretation is not completed merely by studying the historical and literary contexts of a passage. When we read and make our own the prayer texts treated in this volume, we engage in what philosophers and literary theorists have called "the fusion of horizons." As twenty-first-century Christians we approach these texts not only to understand them better, but also in the hope of some kind of personal transformation. The act of reading can be an individual pursuit in the quiet of my room or a communal venture at a liturgy or in a Bible study group. In bringing the ancient historical and literary contexts together with our modern context, we hope that these prayer texts may move our minds and hearts, as they have for believers throughout the centuries.

Daniel Harrington, SJ

Chapter One

Hymns of Praise at Jesus' Birth

In Christian tradition and practice, the hymns of praise in Luke's infancy narrative—the *Magnificat,* the *Benedictus,* the *Gloria,* and the *Nunc Dimittis*—have been taken out of their original literary context and become some of the most common and familiar prayers in our liturgies and private devotions. And well they should! They are great texts—rich and meaningful—and sources of comfort and inspiration to generations of Christians all over the world. However, in keeping with the goals of this book, I want to place them back in their original context in Luke's Gospel and see how they can contribute to a better appreciation of the person of Jesus, his place in the story of our salvation, and his role as the revealer and revelation of the God who creates, sustains, and loves us.

The Lukan Context

Of the four gospels in the New Testament, only two give accounts of Jesus' birth and infancy. Mark starts with the adult Jesus bursting on the scene and proclaiming the coming kingdom of God, while John traces Jesus' origins back to the time before the world's creation ("In the beginning was the Word," John 1:1). Only Matthew 1–2 and Luke 1–2 provide narratives about the birth and infancy of Jesus. Both accounts were written and first read in light of the knowledge of Jesus' achievements as an adult and of faith in the saving significance of Jesus' death and resurrection.

The Matthean and Lukan infancy narratives agree on several important points of fact. They identify Jesus' parents as Mary and Joseph. They place his birth in Bethlehem of Judah, which is David's ancestral home, and explain how the family came to reside in Nazareth of Galilee. But they differ in many of the episodes that they narrate. For example, the visit of the Magi is only in Matthew, and the annunciation and the visitation are only in Luke. They also differ in the characters who receive the most attention and from whose perspective the story is told (Joseph in Matthew, Mary in Luke), and the mood or tone that they convey (conflict in Matthew, peace and joy in Luke).

What often goes unnoticed is how the Matthean and Lukan infancy narratives agree in their basic theological affirmations. They agree that the birth of Jesus marks the decisive moment in the story of our salvation, that Jesus stands in continuity with the great figures in the history of God's people Israel, and that in him God's promises to his people are being fulfilled. In other words, they agree about the ultimate significance of Jesus.

Matthew makes these points first with his genealogy, which places Jesus in line with Abraham, David, and the exile generation. Then he suggests that Jesus' virginal conception fulfilled the prophecy made in Isaiah 7:14 ("a virgin shall conceive," RSV). In chapter 2, Matthew tells how the Magi, as representatives of the nations outside of Israel, came to Bethlehem to pay homage to the divine child. He also shows how Jesus in his infancy followed the pattern set by Moses in Exodus 1–2: location in Egypt, pursuit by the wicked king, and the slaughter of the young children.

In his infancy narrative, Luke uses different characters and episodes to develop the same basic theological affirmations about the child Jesus. One important Lukan device for highlighting the ultimate significance of the child Jesus is the use of hymns of praise uttered by various characters. These hymns are well known by the initial words in their Latin texts: the *Magnificat* (Mary's song); the *Benedictus* (Zechariah's song); the *Gloria* (the angels' song); and the *Nunc Dimittis* (Simeon's song).

All these hymns are prayers of praise to God for having sent Jesus to dwell among us and for making possible a new relationship with God through him. All these hymns use words and phrases from various parts of the Old Testament, but place them now in the new context of the birth of Jesus as the Messiah and Son of David. All of them celebrate his birth, life, death, and resurrection as the fulfillment of God's promises to his people and as the pivotal event in salvation history. Their precise historical origin is not our concern here. Some scholars trace them back to the worship services of the early Palestinian Jewish Christian community, while others view them as adaptations of Jewish hymns or attribute them to Luke the Evangelist. Our main concerns are their literary artistry and theological contents.

MARY'S *Magnificat* (LUKE 1:46-55)

The hymn of praise known as the *Magnificat* takes its traditional title from the first word in the Latin translation. In Luke's infancy narrative, it appears as part of the episode of the visitation (Luke 1:39-56), which follows the announcements of the births of John (1:5-25) and of Jesus (1:26-38). On assenting to become the mother of "the Most High" and the Davidic Messiah, Mary is told that the truth of this promise can be confirmed by the unusual pregnancy of her elderly relative Elizabeth. And so Mary goes from Nazareth in Galilee to visit Elizabeth and Zechariah in the hill country of Judea.

There Mary finds that Elizabeth is indeed going to bear a child. But Elizabeth and her child recognize the superiority of Mary and her child. Like other characters in Luke's infancy narrative, Elizabeth functions as a prophet and declares Mary to be "the mother of my Lord," a title traditionally given to the queen-mother in the ancient Judean royal court. Moreover, Elizabeth identifies Mary as one who has believed God's word and acted upon it—which is how the ideal disciple of Jesus is defined in Luke 8:21 and 11:28.

Although a few ancient manuscripts attribute the *Magnificat* to Elizabeth, in the Lukan context it serves as Mary's witness to what God has done and is doing through her. The Old Testament model for the *Magnificat* is the song of Hannah in 1 Samuel 2:1-10. There Hannah, the childless wife of Elkanah, prays for a child and promises to dedicate him to the Lord. Her vow is accepted, she bears a child, and she brings Samuel to the sanctuary at Shiloh. Her song gives thanks and praise to God for vindicating her trust, answering her prayer, and taking the side of the feeble, hungry, and barren. She goes on to describe how God acts ("he raises up the poor from the dust," 1 Samuel 2:8) and ends with a glimpse of the future king or Messiah: "he [the Lord] will give strength to his king and exalt the power of his anointed" (2:10). Mary's *Magnificat* not only echoes the words and thoughts of Hannah's song but also points toward Jesus as the fulfillment of Israel's hopes for a Davidic Messiah.

[46]And Mary said,
    "My soul magnifies the Lord,
        [47]and my spirit rejoices in God my Savior,
    [48]for he has looked with favor on the lowliness of his
        servant.
    Surely, from now on all generations will call me blessed;

⁴⁹for the Mighty One has done great things for me,
  and holy is his name.
⁵⁰His mercy is for those who fear him
  from generation to generation.
⁵¹He has shown strength with his arm;
  he has scattered the proud in the thoughts of their
    hearts.
⁵²He has brought down the powerful from their thrones,
  and lifted up the lowly;
⁵³he has filled the hungry with good things,
  and sent the rich away empty.
⁵⁴He has helped his servant Israel,
  in remembrance of his mercy,
⁵⁵according to the promise he made to our ancestors,
  to Abraham and to his descendants forever."
(Luke 1:46-55)

In the Lukan context the *Magnificat* praises God on the grounds that Mary's child will bring about a great reversal in human society and the fulfillment of God's promises to Israel. After declaring the greatness of God and expressing her joy (Luke 1:47), she gives the reason for her joy. In her becoming the mother of the Messiah, God has exalted her so that all generations might call her blessed (1:48-50). Then she points to her case as typical of how God deals with humankind; that is, God raises up the lowly and puts down the powerful (1:51-53). Finally she interprets the mercy shown to her as typical of how God deals with Israel as God's covenant people (1:54-55).

A major device in Hebrew poetry is parallelism, and the *Magnificat* is full of parallelisms. In synonymous parallelism the point is made in two similar clauses: "My soul magnifies the Lord, and my spirit rejoices in God my Savior" (Luke 1:46-47). In antithetical parallelism the point is made by two clauses that stand in opposition or contrast: "he has filled the hungry with good things, and sent the rich away empty" (1:53). Another typical poetic device is alternation. Thus there is an alternation between the lowly handmaid and "all generations" (1:48), and the Mighty One and "generation to generation" (1:49-50), to form an ABAB pattern. The antitheses or contrasts in 1:51-53 concern pride, power, and riches, respectively. They combine elements from the reversals in 1 Samuel 2:4-5 and the descriptions of God's actions in 2:6-8.

> [4]The bows of the mighty are broken,
>   but the feeble gird on strength.
> [5]Those who were full have hired themselves out for bread,
>   but those who were hungry are fat with spoil.
> The barren has borne seven,
>   but she who has many children is forlorn.
> [6]The LORD kills and brings to life;
>   he brings down to Sheol and raises up.
> [7]The LORD makes poor and makes rich;
>   he brings low, he also exalts.
> [8]He raises up the poor from the dust;
>   he lifts the needy from the ash heap,
> to make them sit with princes
>   and inherit a seat of honor.
> For the pillars of the earth are the LORD's,
>   and on them he has set the world.
> (1 Samuel 2:4-8)

And the point is rounded off by mention of the promise "to Abraham and his descendants forever" (Luke 1:54-55).

The *Magnificat* develops a triangular relationship among God, the lowly as represented by Mary and Israel, and the proud and powerful. The main actor is God, who is called Lord, Savior, and Mighty One. God shows care for a lowly handmaid, helps Israel, and puts down the proud, powerful, and rich. Mary, the handmaid, praises God and rejoices because she has been blessed by God for her assent to God's plan. She represents the lowly whom God customarily raises up while putting down the high and mighty.

The message of the *Magnificat* is similar to that of the other prayers in Luke's infancy narrative. It is a hymn of praise for what God has done in Christ. It affirms that in Christ, God has acted to save his people, that this salvation is rooted in Israel's history, and that God's promises are being fulfilled.

Zechariah's *Benedictus* (Luke 1:68-79)

The *Benedictus* ("Blessed") takes its traditional title from the first word in the Latin translation. It appears in the setting of the circumcision and naming of John the Baptist (Luke 1:59-66). When both Elizabeth and Zechariah insist that their child should be named John and then suddenly Zechariah is able to speak again after having been struck speechless (1:20, 22), their stunned neighbors ask, "What then will this child become?" (1:66).

In response to their question, Zechariah utters the hymn of praise known as the *Benedictus*. He speaks now under the inspiration of the Holy Spirit, and what he says is identified as prophecy in the twofold sense of speaking on God's behalf and looking into the future. The neighbors' question about John is answered only near the end of the *Benedictus* (Luke 1:76-77). Most of the hymn praises God for the gift of Jesus, the Davidic Messiah.

The structure of the *Benedictus* is similar to that of the *Magnificat*. Zechariah first declares "the Lord God of Israel" worthy of praise ("blessed"), and then explains why ("for") in some detail. There are three great themes that run through the body of the hymn: God's intervention on Israel's behalf, the salvation that God will bring to his people through the Davidic Messiah, and the words in which God has made promises to Israel. These three themes—intervention, salvation, and word—appear in various orders in the four major parts of the hymn (Luke 1:68-70, 71-72, 73-75, and 76-79). The hymn celebrates the birth of Jesus as both the fulfillment of God's promises and God's decisive intervention in the history of salvation. It describes John's role as the precursor of the Davidic Messiah and the preacher of repentance and forgiveness as well as one who waits for the day when Jesus' public ministry will begin.

> [67]Then his father Zechariah was filled with the Holy Spirit and spoke this prophecy:
>> [68]"Blessed be the Lord God of Israel,
>>> for he has looked favorably on his people and redeemed them.
>> [69]He has raised up a mighty savior for us
>>> in the house of his servant David,
>> [70]as he spoke through the mouth of his holy prophets from of old,
>>> [71]that we would be saved from our enemies and
>>> from the hand of all who hate us.
>> [72]Thus he has shown the mercy promised to our ancestors,
>>> and has remembered his holy covenant,
>> [73]the oath that he swore to our ancestor Abraham,
>>> to grant us [74]that we, being rescued from the hands of our enemies,

might serve him without fear, [75]in holiness and
        righteousness
    before him all our days.
[76]And you, child, will be called the prophet of the Most
        High;
    for you will go before the Lord to prepare his ways,
[77]to give knowledge of salvation to his people
    by the forgiveness of their sins.
[78]By the tender mercy of our God,
    the dawn from on high will break upon us,
[79]to give light to those who sit in darkness and in the
        shadow of death,
    to guide our feet into the way of peace."
(Luke 1:67-79)

The main character in the first section of the hymn (Luke 1:68-70) is described as "the Lord God of Israel." This title is part of a major theme running through the hymn; that is, the salvation being proclaimed in the hymn is deeply rooted in Israel's past. The reasons for God's being acknowledged as worthy of praise include God's intervention on Israel's behalf ("he has looked favorably on his people"); God's raising up the Davidic Messiah as Israel's savior; and his fidelity to his word spoken through the "holy prophets," perhaps most concretely by Nathan in 2 Samuel 7:12-16:

[12]When your days are fulfilled and you lie down with your ancestors, I will raise up your offspring after you, who shall come forth from your body, and I will establish his kingdom. [13]He shall build a house for my name, and I will establish the throne of his kingdom forever. [14]I will be a father to him, and he shall be a son to me. When he commits iniq-

uity, I will punish him with a rod such as mortals use, with blows inflicted by human beings. [15]But I will not take my steadfast love from him, as I took it from Saul, whom I put away from before you. [16]Your house and your kingdom shall be made sure forever before me; your throne shall be established forever.
(2 Samuel 7:12-16)

The hymn, then, is clearly more about Jesus than about John the Baptist.

In the second and third sections (Luke 1:71-72 and 1:73-75), the focus of attention shifts from God to the people ("we"). The speaker regards himself and his group as representing Israel, the people of God. In the second section, he refers to God's saving actions in the exodus from Egypt ("saved from our enemies and from the hand of all who hate us," see Psalm 106:10) and in making the "holy covenant" at Mount Sinai, thus evoking the memory of Moses to go along with that of David. The third section links the themes of divine intervention and salvation to the promise made to Abraham that his offspring would become a great nation (see Genesis 12:2; 22:17-18) and so able to serve God "in holiness and righteousness" (Luke 1:75). Thus the child Jesus is not only the Davidic Messiah but also the one in whom God's promises made to Moses and Abraham will be fulfilled.

In the fourth section, the focus moves first to John the Baptist ("And you, child") in Luke 1:76-77 and then to Jesus the Davidic Messiah again ("the dawn from on high") in 1:78-79. The description of John reinforces his subordination to Jesus and develops a characteristic theme of Luke's infancy narrative: John is great, but Jesus is even greater. Whereas Jesus was previously identified as "the Son of the Most High" (1:32), John is called "the prophet of the Most High" (1:76) Likewise, John is the one who prepares "the way of the Lord" and who proclaims the forgiveness of sins (see Luke 3:3-4). What "this child" named John will become is the forerunner or precursor of Jesus the Davidic Messiah. The subject of Luke 1:78-79 seems once more to be Jesus and what he will do on behalf of God's people. As the living expression of God's mercy, Jesus the Davidic Messiah will bring light to those who dwell in darkness and will set God's people on "the way of peace" (1:79).

According to Luke 1:80, when John grew up, he went off to "the wilderness," which most likely means the Judean desert. That area had become a hotbed for Jewish religious movements in this period. The Jewish group—commonly identified as Essenes—that lived a kind of monastic existence at Qumran near the Dead Sea is one example. Qumran was where the major discovery of Dead Sea scrolls took place in the late 1940s. Whether John was a member of this group or some other group in the general area is not certain. At any rate, John eventually developed his own movement, practiced the rite of baptism as preparation for the coming kingdom of God, and attracted disciples and large crowds. But the Evangelists all insist that although John was great and was the one who baptized Jesus, as the Davidic Messiah and Son of the Most High, Jesus was even greater. That is precisely the message that John's father Zechariah conveys in this hymn.

THE ANGELS' *Gloria* (LUKE 2:14)

The angels' song of praise at the birth of Jesus in Luke 2:14 provides the beginning of the Christian hymn known as the *Gloria* that is recited or sung at Sunday and holy day Masses. It marks the birth

of Jesus as the moment when heaven and earth join together to celebrate the glory of God. The context in which the hymn appears
(Luke 2:8-20) highlights Jesus' identity as the Davidic Messiah.

According to Luke 2:1-7, Jesus' birth took place in Bethlehem,
the birthplace of King David. David himself was a shepherd, and
in the Old Testament Bethlehem is known as "the tower of the
flock" (Genesis 35:21; Micah 4:8). The angels proclaim to the
shepherds in the area surrounding Bethlehem that this newborn
child born in the city of David is the Messiah of Jewish expectations (Luke 2:11). At the same time, their proclamation uses
language associated with the Roman emperor: "good news . . .
Savior . . . Lord." Thus the child Jesus fulfills the divine promise of a Messiah-like David and possesses a dignity like that of,
or superior to, the emperor. Jesus' birth, despite its humble circumstances, is a great moment in Israel's history and indeed in
world history.

The angels' hymn of praise to the shepherds illustrates the parallelism that is characteristic of Hebrew poetry:

> [14]"Glory to God in the highest heaven,
>   and on earth peace among those whom he favors!"
> (Luke 2:14)

The birth of the child Jesus is both the occasion to ascribe glory
to God and a time to enjoy perfect fullness or harmony ("peace"
in the root sense of *shalom*) on earth. The older and perhaps more
familiar translation of the second part of the verse ("and on earth
peace, among men good will") rests on inferior Greek manuscript
evidence. Moreover, a Hebrew phrase found in several texts among
the Dead Sea scrolls ("the elect of his [God's] favor") confirms the
wording of the better manuscripts ("and on earth peace among

those whom he [God] favors"). The second part of the verse identifies the shepherds as the privileged recipients of divine favor or grace. In Jesus' time, shepherds were certainly not high-status persons, but they are the kind of people to whom the angels publicly proclaim the birth of Jesus, the Son of David and the Messiah. The real presence of God is now in Bethlehem with this child. The *Gloria* reminds us that the birth of Jesus has implications and even reverberations both in heaven and on earth.

Simeon's *Nunc Dimittis* (Luke 2:29-32)

The short hymn of praise uttered by Simeon in the Jerusalem Temple is traditionally called the *Nunc Dimittis* ("Now you are dismissing"), from the first two words in the Latin translation. It too marks the birth of Jesus as a climactic moment in salvation history and places it in the context of Israel's story as the people of God.

The narrative context is the series of events following the birth of Jesus. In accordance with the Old Testament Law, Jesus is named and circumcised on the eighth day (Leviticus 12:3) and is brought to the Temple as the firstborn male child for "presentation" to the Lord (Exodus 13:2, 12, 15). And his mother submits to the ritual of "purification" forty days after childbirth and offers the appropriate sacrifices at the Temple (Leviticus 12:1-8). By undergoing these rituals, Jesus the Messiah shows himself to be in perfect solidarity with his people.

These rituals of presentation and purification provide the occasion for Simeon to utter his hymn of praise. Described as "righteous and devout" (Luke 2:25), he is precisely the kind of person who can recognize who the child Jesus is and what he represents. Moreover, because the Holy Spirit rests upon him, what Simeon says amounts to a prophecy. His hope was to see and experience "the consolation of Israel" (2:25), a phrase that echoes the first words of what is called Second Isaiah ("Comfort, O comfort my people, says your God," Isaiah 40:1). According to Luke 2:26, Simeon had been promised that he would see "the Lord's Messiah" before his death. The *Nunc Dimittis* is his response to having taken the infant Jesus in his arms and recognizing that the child was the answer to God's promise to him and thus the consolation of Israel.

> [29]"Master, now you are dismissing your servant in peace,
>   according to your word;
> [30]for my eyes have seen your salvation,
>   [31]which you have prepared in the presence of all
>   peoples,
> [32]a light for revelation to the Gentiles
>   and for glory to your people Israel."
> (Luke 2:29-32)

In this short hymn of praise, Simeon in Luke 2:29 addresses God as "Master," which is an unusual divine title in the New Testament. He characterizes himself as God's servant or slave and observes that he can now die in peace. In Luke 2:30-32 he gives the reason why ("for") in terms that echo phrases from Isaiah 40–55. That part of the Book of Isaiah, called Second Isaiah, seems to have been composed in 537 B.C. or so, in the community of Jewish exiles in Babylon. The political and religious leaders of Judah had been brought there by the Babylonians in the early sixth century B.C. With the conquest of Babylon by the Persian king, Cyrus, permission had been given for them to return home and rebuild the Jerusalem Temple.

Second Isaiah is a collection of hymns or prophetic discourses that sought to encourage the exiles to go back home. In its literary artistry and theological profundity, Second Isaiah is surely one of the high points of the Hebrew Bible. It identifies the God of Israel as the Creator and Lord of the universe, claims that Israel has paid double for all its sins, and promises that the return home will amount to a new creation and a new exodus. However, the reality that was the return home did not meet all the expectations aroused by the prophet. (See Third Isaiah, chapters 56–66, and the books of Haggai, Zechariah, Ezra, and Nehemiah for descriptions of the mixed results that accompanied the return from exile.)

Nevertheless, the extravagant hopes and promises contained in Second Isaiah remained alive and became part of Israel's Scriptures. More than five hundred years later, Jews like Simeon were hoping that they might at last see the consolation of Israel promised by the prophet. Both the Qumran community, where the Dead Sea scrolls were found, and the early Christians, as they are represented in the New Testament, showed a special interest in Second Isaiah. They saw its promises being fulfilled in the history and life of their movements.

The reason why Simeon praises God in Luke 2:30-32 is the perception that God's promises to Israel in Second Isaiah were being fulfilled in Jesus. His words in 2:30-31 about his now having seen God's salvation prepared in the presence of all peoples echo what is said in Isaiah 52:10: "The LORD has bared his holy arm / before the eyes of all the nations; / and all the ends of the earth shall see / the salvation of our God." His declaration of Jesus as "a light of revelation to the Gentiles" in Luke 2:32 recalls the vocation of God's Servant in Isaiah 42:6 and 49:6 ("a light to the nations"), and his role as "glory to your people Israel" alludes to Isaiah 46:13 ("I will put salvation in Zion, for Israel my glory").

The message of Simeon's *Nunc Dimittis* is that the salvation promised to God's people in Isaiah 40–55 as they returned from exile was finally being fulfilled in the person of Jesus. The witness of Simeon is confirmed by the appearance of the prophet Anna, who also praises God and finds in the child Jesus "the redemption of Jerusalem" (Luke 2:38). The joy surrounding the prophecies of Simeon and Anna is softened somewhat by Simeon's further prophecy about Jesus' future role as the point of decision among his own people and as the object of hostility ("a sign that will be opposed," 2:34) and suffering ("a sword will pierce your own soul too," 2:35). In the context of Luke's two-volume work, Simeon's prayer places Jesus in the framework of Israel's history and life ("for glory to your people Israel," 2:32) and the church's mission to carry the gospel to all nations ("a light for revelation to the Gentiles," 2:32). These two themes, of course, correspond to the scope of Luke's Gospel and his Acts of the Apostles.

BRINGING THE CONTEXTS TOGETHER

The four hymnic pieces in Luke 1–2 represent the so-called anthological style. All of these texts use words and images from the Old Testament and other Jewish prayers to celebrate the new thing that God has done in the birth of Jesus the Messiah. They all point to this event as a pivotal moment in the history of Israel and in world history. Their texts have been set to music many times throughout the centuries. As hymns in praise of God and his Messiah, they breathe the spirit of joy. In the liturgical cycle we associate them with Advent (*Magnificat, Benedictus*), Christmas (*Gloria*), and the Presentation (*Nunc Dimittis*).

These hymnic compositions can provide many themes for personal prayer and meditation. The *Magnificat* highlights Mary's greatness in agreeing to become the mother of the Messiah, celebrates God's surprising preference for weak and unlikely human instruments to serve as vehicles for his saving plan, and recalls God's remarkable fidelity to the promises made to his people. The *Benedictus* praises God for his faithfulness to the covenant and his mercy toward his people, and points to Jesus as the fulfillment of the divine promises and to John the Baptist as the one who will prepare the way for the Messiah. The *Gloria* points to the birth of Jesus the Messiah as an event encompassing heaven and earth in its significance, and as a proof of divine favor or grace. In the *Nunc Dimittis,* Simeon, the prophet and symbol of the faithful among God's people, recognizes the significance of the child Jesus for Israel and for all the nations.

The Lukan hymns point us not so much inward toward ourselves and our concerns, but rather outward and upward toward the faithful and merciful God, and to Jesus as the Messiah of Israel and the Son of the Most High (see Luke 1:35).

Think, Pray, and Act

Take stock of your own prayer life, and consider how the hymns of praise in Luke's infancy narrative might enrich your appreciation of Jesus and your own way of praying.

Think
🔖 Write a description of when and how you pray. Does it amount to a serious prayer life? Is there room for praise as well as petition? How might you improve the quality and quantity of your prayer life?

§ How often do you praise God for what God has done in Jesus? How often do you praise God for what God has done and is doing in your life?

§ To what extent do you use the language of the Bible in your prayer? Is this helpful, or does it present a barrier at times?

Pray

§ Spend a few minutes slowly and meditatively reading the *Magnificat*. What links do you find with your own experiences? What do you want to say to God on the basis of these prayers?

§ Repeat the exercise with the *Benedictus*. What is the same, and what is different?

Act

§ Set aside some time each day in your prayer to praise God, especially for the gift of Christ to us and for what God has done for you through Christ.

Chapter Two

Jesus and Prayer in His Jewish Context

T he Word became flesh and lived among us" (John 1:14). Christianity is an incarnational religion. We believe that God, in the person of Jesus of Nazareth, took on our humanity in the land of Israel in what we call the first century A.D. As we learn from the gospels, Jesus made his own the language, literary forms, and theological themes of Jewish prayer of his time. Jesus' prayers and teachings on prayer as we find them in the gospels fit well within this historical and literary context. At the same time, they point to him as not only a wise and challenging teacher but also as a distinctive and even unique figure, one worthy of such titles as "Son of God" and "Our Lord Jesus Christ."

JEWISH PRAYER IN JESUS' TIME

Jesus' teaching about prayer and his practice are deeply rooted in the Jewish tradition as expressed in the biblical Book of Psalms and in the prayers of Jews throughout the centuries. His direct address to God, his praise of God's work in creation and salvation history, and his emphasis on the prayer of petition were—and are—major elements in the Jewish prayer tradition.

The Book of Psalms consists of 150 prayers, ranging from a few short verses to the 176 verses in the elaborately structured Psalm 119. The present book is a collection of earlier collections and looks something like a hymnal. Many of these psalms were first composed for use in worship services held in the Jerusalem Temple. Some psalms were obviously intended to accompany the offering of sacrifices, whereas other psalms, such as Psalm 119, are more meditative and were perhaps designed for use in other communal and personal contexts.

In studying and praying the psalms, it is important to recognize the different categories or scripts. The Hebrew word for the psalms is *Tehillim,* which means "praises." While all the psalms sing God's praises in some way or other, the largest category is the lament. In these psalms, the individual or community addresses God with some complaint, expresses trust in God, and hopes that God will do something about the problem. There are psalms of confidence in God and thanksgiving to God as well as celebrations of God's actions in creation and in Israel's history. There are also wisdom psalms, songs of Zion about Jerusalem and its Temple, and royal psalms about the king or about God as king.

By Jesus' time, the Book of Psalms had become the prayer book of the Jewish people. The many manuscripts of the psalms in the library of the community at Qumran, which gave us the most important of the Dead Sea scrolls, indicate how popular they were. The psalms not only served as prayers to be read and recited but also provided the language and theology for writing new prayers and hymns. The Jewish prayers composed in Jesus' time drew freely on the words and images in the biblical psalms and placed them in new combinations and new contexts. To a large extent the biblical Book of Psalms shaped the language and theology of Jewish prayer in Jesus' time.

Also by Jesus' time, what has now become the traditional order of Jewish prayer was beginning to take shape. An observant Jewish male is expected to recite the "Eighteen Benedictions" three times a day. Those prayers are accompanied in the morning and evening by the recitation of three biblical passages (Deuteronomy 6:4-9; 11:13-21; Numbers 15:37-41) plus opening and closing benedictions. These readings are called the *Shema*, the Hebrew word for "hear," which is the first word in the text of Deuteronomy 6:4 ("Hear, O Israel"). It is likely that Jesus and his first followers were familiar with something like this routine of worship. In fact, Jesus may have intended the Lord's Prayer (Matthew 6:9-13; Luke 11:2-4) as a simplified version of the Eighteen Benedictions. This suggestion is strengthened by the notice in the *Didache* (8:3), an early handbook for Christian life, that the Lord's Prayer was to be recited three times a day.

The theological framework of the Jewish daily prayer is set by the opening words of the Shema: "Hear, O Israel, the Lord our God, the Lord is one" (see Deuteronomy 6:4). The proper human response is to "love the LORD your God with all your heart and with all your soul and with all your might" (Deuteronomy 6:5). The opening and concluding benedictions ("Blessed are you, Lord our God, King of the universe") praise God for his work of creation and redemption and for revealing his will to his people.

The "Eighteen Benedictions" constitute the core of the Jewish daily prayer. They are sometimes called *Tephillah,* which is the Hebrew word for "prayer," because they form the Jewish prayer *par excellence.* They are also referred to as the *Amidah,* from the Hebrew word for "stand up," since they are recited while standing. They are properly recited in a group of ten men, but may be said individually if it is not possible to find the right number or *minyan* in Hebrew. Women are not obligated to pray three times a day, since their domestic duties might make their participation impossible. Each man recites the prayers individually and at his own pace, allowing for differences in devotion or attention. The prayers have a fixed form. But individuals may expand the prayers or make minor substitutions.

The Eighteen Benedictions are in fact a combination of praises and petitions (See Joseph Heinemann with Jakob J. Petuchowski, *Literature of the Synagogue,* pp. 33–36). The first three benedictions address God as both the God of the patriarchs Abraham, Isaac, and Jacob and the creator of heaven and earth; as the powerful and eternal one who revives the dead; and as the holy one whose name is awesome. The first set of petitions (four through nine) concerns personal matters in the present: understanding, repentance, forgiveness, redemption, healing, and abundant harvests. The second set (ten through fifteen) expresses national concerns about Israel's future: the gathering of the dispersed Israelites, just leaders, no hope for apostates, compassion for converts, the rebuilding of Jerusalem, the coming of the Davidic Messiah, and the hearing of prayers. The final three benedictions concern reverent worship of God, thanksgiving to God, and peace.

These Jewish prayers have been composed and practiced in a theological framework that is typical not only of Jewish prayer but also of the prayers that we find in the New Testament and the Christian tradition. These Jewish prayers balance the transcendence of God as Creator and Lord with the immanence of God, who may be addressed directly and who can and does enter into human affairs. Most of the phrases come from the Hebrew Bible, but now appear in new combinations and new contexts. There is a fixed form but also room for individual expression and adaptation. And there is both a sense of community (the proper number or *minyan* for the prayer to be "official") and a respect for individual persons praying at their own pace and according to their own devotion.

Another Jewish prayer that is essential for understanding Jesus' own prayer is called the *Kaddish*, from the Hebrew word for "holy." While in the Jewish tradition it has become associated with the death of a loved one, in its content it is a prayer for the coming of the kingdom of God. The *Kaddish* asks that God's name be sanctified or "hallowed" by all creation and that God's kingdom be fully established soon and in our lifetime:

> May his great name be magnified and sanctified in the world that is to be created anew, when he will revive the dead and raise them up unto life eternal, rebuild the city of Jerusalem, and establish his temple in the midst thereof, and uproot all alien worship from the earth and restore the worship of the true God. May the Holy One, blessed be he, establish his kingdom and his glory during your life and during your days, and during the life of all the house of Israel, speedily and at a near time; and say Amen. (Heinemann, p. 84)

The parallels between the *Kaddish* and the Lord's Prayer are striking. Whether Jesus was alluding to the *Kaddish* or something like it, is not certain. But there is clearly a kinship in wording and content between them, which suggests once more that the prayers included in the New Testament must be understood in the context of contemporary Judaism.

THE LORD'S PRAYER

Many Christians are not aware that there are two different versions of the Lord's Prayer in the New Testament. The more familiar version (Matthew 6:9-13) appears in the Sermon on the Mount. A somewhat shorter version (Luke 11:2-4) is part of

Jesus' first instruction about prayer in Luke's Gospel (11:1-13) during his long journey with his disciples from Galilee to Jerusalem. Both versions are prayers for the full coming of God's kingdom. Both versions were used in early Christian communities—Matthew's version by Jewish Christians, and Luke's version by Gentile Christians.

Since the Lukan version is less familiar, it may be a better starting point. According to Luke 11:1, Jesus composed this prayer in response to a request from a disciple to give his followers a prayer like the one John the Baptist had apparently given to his followers. We do not have the text of John's prayer. But from everything we know about John (see Luke 3:1-20), it must have concerned the full coming of God's kingdom.

> [2]He said to them, "When you pray, say:
> Father, hallowed be your name.
>> Your kingdom come.
>> [3]Give us each day our daily bread.
> [4]And forgive us our sins,
>> for we ourselves forgive everyone indebted to us.
> And do not bring us to the time of trial."
> (Luke 11:2-4)

The Lukan version of the Lord's Prayer is addressed simply to God as "Father." This title seems to reflect Jesus' characteristic way of speaking to God and his consciousness of his own special relationship with God as the "Son of God." By teaching his followers to call upon God as their "Father" too, Jesus invites them—and us—to share in his relationship of intimacy with God. In the ancient Mediterranean world, a father was expected to care for and form his children into adults. And in turn, children were expected to show respect and honor toward their father. Paul affirms that all Christians who have received the Holy Spirit in baptism can cry out to God with the words "Abba, Father" (Galatians 4:6; *Abba* is the Aramaic word for Father), and regard themselves as children of God alongside Jesus.

The body of the Lord's Prayer is a prayer of petition. It contains two petitions for the full coming of God's kingdom (Luke 11:2) that use second-person singular language ("your name . . . your kingdom") and three petitions for sustenance, forgiveness, and protection during the kingdom's coming (11:3-4) that are cast in first-person plural language ("give us . . . forgive us . . . do not bring us").

The two "you" petitions concern what was the central theme of Jesus' own preaching and activity: the kingdom of God. Most of Jesus' parables and many of his other teachings challenged his hearers to discern the presence of God's kingdom among them and to look forward in hope to its future fullness. His many healings and exorcisms are best understood as previews or anticipations of the fullness of God's kingdom.

In Luke 11:2 the focus is on the future dimension of the kingdom. Here Jesus teaches us to pray that one day all creation may join in a cosmic chorus in praise of God as sovereign lord over all. In that way God's name will be "hallowed." The second "you" petition is parallel to the first: "Your kingdom come." While God's kingdom has been made present in and through Jesus, the fullness is yet to come. Like the Jewish *Kaddish* prayer, the Lord's Prayer looks forward to the establishment of God's perfect reign soon.

The three "we" petitions concern what we need if we are to enter and enjoy God's kingdom when it comes in its fullness. Jews in Jesus' time expected that the coming of the kingdom would be a time of testing and trial for humankind. Some texts (including Mark 13:8) describe this period as the "birth pangs" or "woes" of the Messiah. While for wise and righteous persons this time will end in their vindication and reward, it will nonetheless involve suffering and danger.

The three "we" petitions in Luke 11:3-4 must be interpreted in this context. We need for God to sustain us by providing us with "our daily bread." We need also for God to forgive our sins. And we can receive such divine forgiveness provided that we too are willing to forgive those who are "indebted" to us. Whether "indebted" is to be taken in its financial sense or spiritually or both is not clear. In some Jewish circles, "debt" had become a metaphor for sin as an offense against God and/or other people. The third and last "we" petition ("and do not bring us to the time of trial") is difficult to translate and interpret. It asks God to spare us the worst of the testing and to help us not to fall in whatever trial might come our way.

The more familiar Matthean version of the Lord's Prayer (6:9-13) adapts the opening address to the more common Jewish title for God in prayer, "Our Father in heaven." The pronominal adjective "our" alludes to God's presence among us (God's immanence), while "in heaven" reminds us of the cosmic scope of God's reign (God's transcendence). The third "you" petition ("Your will be done, on earth as it is in heaven," 6:10) is parallel to the petitions about the hallowing of God's name and the full coming of God's kingdom. The "we" petition about forgiveness uses the image of "debt" twice ("our debts . . . our debtors"). Again it is not clear whether "debt" is meant on the financial or spiritual level. And the final "we" petition is expanded by the parallel clause "rescue us from the evil one" (6:13) The "evil one" may refer to Satan as the "tester" (see Job 1–2). Or it may simply be a way of referring to "evil" in general. The expanded address and the added petition are typical of the flexibility of Jewish prayer and may reflect the use of the Lord's Prayer in Jewish Christian communities.

The Lord's Prayer has deep roots in contemporary Jewish prayers, as we have seen from the psalms, the Eighteen Benedictions, and the *Kaddish*. And yet it fits perfectly with what we know about the teachings and activities of Jesus himself. As we learn from the *Didache,* it soon became the characteristic prayer of early Christians. Its different versions in Matthew 6:9-13 and Luke 11:2-4 attest to its use in both Jewish and Gentile Christian circles. The Lord's Prayer is an expression of our intimacy with and dependence on God, of our hope for the full coming of God's kingdom, and of our need for God's sustenance, forgiveness, and protection in the meantime.

PERSISTENCE IN PRAYER

The Lord's Prayer is a prayer of petition. In form and content it is similar to the Jewish Eighteen Benedictions and the *Kaddish.* Its shorter Lukan version appears as the initial part in the first of two blocks of Jesus' teachings about how to pray (see Luke 11:1-13; 18:1-14). Both of those blocks concern the prayer of petition and urge us to be persistent, bold, and humble in our prayers.

Jesus' parable of the friend at midnight (11:5-8) reflects a common experience:

> [5]And he said to them, "Suppose one of you has a friend, and you go to him at midnight and say to him, 'Friend, lend me three loaves of bread; [6]for a friend of mine has arrived, and I have nothing to set before him.' [7]And he answers from within, 'Do not bother me; the door has already been

locked, and my children are with me in bed; I cannot get up and give you anything.' ⁸I tell you, even though he will not get up and give him anything because he is his friend, at least because of his persistence he will get up and give him whatever he needs."
(Luke 11:5-8)

Often a friend or family member, especially a child, will be so persistent in making a request that we find it easier to give in rather than to continue to resist. We grow weary of hearing, "Please, please, please . . ." The surprising point of this parable is that if we are persistent enough and bold enough in prayer, God, like a worn-down parent, will eventually give into our petitions and grant our requests.

Jesus continues the surprises by insisting on the almost automatic efficacy of prayers of petition in Luke 11:9-10: "Ask, and it will be given you; search, and you will find; knock, and the door will be opened for you." Here there are no theological qualifications (if it be God's will) or conditions (if the request is made sincerely, or if it is good for you). The absolute character of the saying further encourages us to boldness and persistence in prayer. There are no "ifs, ands, or buts" about it.

The first Lukan block of Jesus' teachings on prayer is concluded in 11:11-13 with two more short parables. If your child asked for a fish, would you give him a snake? Or if your child asked for an egg, would you give her a scorpion? Of course not! Any parent and any adult in their right minds would give only good gifts to their own children. Then using the logical and rhetorical device of arguing "from the lesser to the greater" that was used extensively by the rabbinic sages, Jesus says, "How much more will the heavenly Father give the Holy Spirit to those who ask him!" (11:13). Beside confirming us in being bold and persistent in prayer, this saying affirms that God wants to hear and answer our prayers and to give us good gifts, and that God especially wants to give us the best gift of all—the Holy Spirit. The gift of the Holy Spirit will enable us to enter into the divine life and live out of the power of the Spirit of God.

The second Lukan instruction on the prayer of petition in 18:1-14 reinforces the theme of persistence in prayer (18:1-8) and insists on the importance of humility in prayer (18:9-14). The parable of the persistent widow is prefaced by the notice that Jesus told this parable about the "need to pray always and not to lose heart."

> [1]Then Jesus told them a parable about their need to pray always and not to lose heart. [2]He said, "In a certain city there was a judge who neither feared God nor had respect for people. [3]In that city there was a widow who kept coming to him and saying, 'Grant me justice against my opponent.' [4]For a while he refused; but later he said to himself, 'Though I have no fear of God and no respect for anyone, [5]yet because this widow keeps bothering me, I will grant her justice, so that she may not wear me out by continually coming.'" [6]And the Lord said, "Listen to what the unjust judge says. [7]And will not God grant justice to his chosen ones who cry to him day and night? Will he delay long in helping them? [8]I tell you, he will quickly grant justice to them. And yet, when the Son of Man comes, will he find faith on earth?"
> (Luke 18:1-8)

The parable features two characters: a widow and a judge. In the ancient world, a widow was among the most defenseless and powerless persons. Unless she had adult sons who were powerful and influential, a widow had no social standing and no political power. The other character is a judge, who in this case is an opportunist and a pragmatist, without respect for God or other persons. One might presume that nothing good could come from their interaction. But when the widow brings her case, she eventually prevails. She prevails not because she is influential or powerful and not because the judge is honest or compassionate. Rather, she wins her case only because she is persistent. She keeps after the judge and finally wears him down. Because the widow will not take no for an answer, the judge decides to give her what she wants in the hope of getting rid of her. The point of Jesus' parable is clear. If a defenseless and powerless widow can wear down a corrupt judge through her persistence alone, how much more can we expect that God, the just and merciful judge, will hear our prayers and answer them positively if we persist?

But how can we pray always? Persistence is one thing, but praying always is something even more. When we hear the word "prayer," most of us instinctively think of formal prayers like the Lord's Prayer or the Rosary. And we should, since formal prayers are integral to Christian spirituality. There is, however, another way of thinking about prayer in Christian life. It is the effort to make our whole life into a prayer—that is, to pray always. This kind of prayer involves offering all that we are and have and do to the service of God, recalling God's presence at various times during our day, and making all our personal encounters and actions into a kind of prayer. This form of prayer means bringing all our successes and failures, joys and sorrows, highs and lows to God in prayer. This habit of prayer, of course, needs to be complemented by formal prayers. But the combination of the two can add up to praying always.

HUMILITY IN PRAYER

The parable of the Pharisee and the tax collector in Luke 18:9-14 reminds us that God hears the prayers of some surprising persons, and that we all must approach God in prayer with humility.

[9]He also told this parable to some who trusted in themselves that they were righteous and regarded others with contempt: [10] "Two men went up to the temple to pray, one a Pharisee and the other a tax collector. [11]The Pharisee, standing by himself, was praying thus, 'God, I thank you that I am not like other people: thieves, rogues, adulterers, or even like this tax collector. [12]I fast twice a week; I give a tenth of all my income.' [13]But the tax collector, standing far off, would not even look up to heaven, but was beating his breast and saying, 'God, be merciful to me, a sinner!' [14]I tell you, this man went down to his home justified rather than the other; for all who exalt themselves will be humbled, but all who humble themselves will be exalted."
(Luke 18:9-14)

To appreciate this parable and its message, we must place the two main characters in their historical and social context in first-century Palestine. In the gospels, the Pharisees often appear as negative characters. They are the most persistent opponents of Jesus, and he often criticizes their attitudes and behavior. In English today, the term "Pharisee" can refer to a legalist imposing strict views on others while really being a religious hypocrite or fraud, someone who pretends to be devout and observant but really is not.

In Jesus' context, however, people would have heard the word differently. The Pharisees were members of a prominent and generally well-respected Jewish religious movement. Many of them were genuinely devout and observant. They were the progressives of their day, seeking to adapt biblical laws to changed historical circumstances and to the demands of their everyday life. They gathered regularly for prayer and study, and their common meals celebrated their group identity and religious commitment. Of all the Jewish groups of Jesus' time, Jesus was closest to them. He shared an agenda with them, debated with them, and sometimes agreed with them. For example, Jesus and the Pharisees agreed about the resurrection of the dead. Those who first heard Jesus' parable would have considered the Pharisee as an exemplar of Jewish learning and piety.

In Jesus' time and place, the tax collector in the parable would have been regarded as the opposite of the Pharisee. Taxes were often let out for bid. The Roman government official or the agent for Herod Antipas might specify the amount to be collected from the inhabitants of a certain area. The tax collector would then contract to pay the specified amount to the government. What he collected above and beyond that amount was his to keep. So in Jesus' day, tax collectors were suspect on two counts. They were suspected of dishonesty for overcharging the people and keeping the excess profits for themselves. They were also suspected of being collaborators and instruments of the Roman occupiers.

These two men went up to the Temple to pray. Whose prayer was heard by God? And why? The Pharisee's prayer was not heard because he exalted himself. His prayer was so focused on himself, his superiority to the tax collector, and his own spiritual achievements that it was hardly a prayer at all. It was more like an exercise in self-congratulation than prayer. By contrast, the tax collector, whatever his failings may have been, knew who God is and who he was before God. And so he prayed simply and sincerely, "God, be merciful to me, a sinner."

Whose prayer does God hear? If our prayer becomes an exercise in self-congratulation like that of the Pharisee, our prayer will not be heard because it is not prayer at all. However, if our prayer celebrates God's justice and mercy, if it acknowledges our dependence on God, our sinfulness, and our need for God's mercy, then God will hear our prayer, because it is genuine prayer made in a spirit of humility proper to us as God's creatures and servants.

JESUS' PRACTICE OF AND TEACHINGS ABOUT PRAYER

The gospels tell us surprisingly little about Jesus' routine or regular practice of prayer. In what seems to have been the earliest gospel, Mark notes that after Jesus' initial successes in calling disciples, casting out a demon, and healing Peter's mother-in-law and many other sick people, Jesus got up early in the morning and went to pray at a deserted place (1:35). He prayed there until he was summoned by Simon Peter and his companions to resume his public ministry of proclaiming God's kingdom. According to Mark 6:46, Jesus withdrew to a mountain to pray in between the miraculous feeding of the five thousand and his walking on the waters of the Sea of Galilee. In the Old Testament, both the desert and the mountain sometimes serve as special places for encountering God. One gets the impression from Mark's very few notices about Jesus' prayer life that he had developed a rhythm between his communion with the Father and his teaching and other public activities.

In the teaching material in Mark 11:25, Jesus advises a willingness to forgive others if we wish to be forgiven by God: "Whenever you stand praying, forgive, if you have anything against anyone;

so that your Father in heaven may also forgive you your trespasses." This echoes the words of the Lord's Prayer (see Matthew 6:12 and Luke 11:4). And in Mark 13:18, Jesus describes the events preceding the coming of the Son of Man and warns his disciples to "pray that it may not be in winter," when traveling would be especially difficult.

In his revised and expanded version of Mark's Gospel, Matthew notes that Jesus went up the mountain by himself to pray (14:23) before walking on the water. To Mark's warning to pray about not having to flee in winter, Matthew in 24:20 adds "or on a sabbath." Thus, for his largely Jewish Christian community, he addresses what might have posed a crisis of conscience of having to violate the Sabbath in order to flee. To Mark's account of Jesus blessing the children (Mark 10:13-15), Matthew in 19:13 specifies that Jesus was asked to "pray" over them.

In Matthew's Sermon on the Mount (chapters 5–7), Jesus challenges his followers to love their enemies and "pray for those who persecute you" (5:44). In the section (6:1-18) devoted to the three acts of piety expected of pious Jewish men (almsgiving, prayer, and fasting), Jesus insists that they be performed without ostentation or public display. He does not want them to be done only to get a reputation for holiness, but rather as genuine works of religious devotion to God. In discussing prayer in 6:5-6, Jesus first criticizes as "hypocrites" those who pray only at synagogues or in the streets to be seen by others, and warns that "they have received their reward." By contrast, he tells his followers to pray in places where they cannot be seen ("go into your room and shut the door") on the grounds that there will be no mixed motives in that kind of prayer. Acts of piety like prayer are intended to express one's devotion to God and should be kept as pure and authentic as possible. In Matthew 6:7-8, Jesus goes

on to warn against long and wordy prayers "as the Gentiles do."
He observes that "your Father knows what you need before you
ask him." These teachings set the stage for the text of the Lord's
Prayer, which as we have seen seems to be a compact version of
the Eighteen Benedictions.

At one pivotal point in Matthew's narrative (11:25-26), we
have a prayer of thanksgiving recited by Jesus. Much of Matthew
11 and 12 is devoted to the mixed reception and even hostility
that Jesus and his message of God's kingdom were receiving from
his Jewish contemporaries. In the midst of this generally gloomy
account, there is a ray of light and hope when Jesus thanks God
for those persons who had surprisingly received him and his message in a positive way.

> [25]At that time Jesus said, "I thank you, Father, Lord of
> heaven and earth, because you have hidden these things
> from the wise and the intelligent and have revealed them to
> infants; [26]yes, Father, for such was your gracious will."
> (Matthew 11:25-26)

Here Jesus' prayer takes the form of a thanksgiving. In the Old
Testament and in other Jewish prayers, a thanksgiving was a public
witness and affirmation that God had been at work in rescuing the
speaker from great danger or in revealing some important truth.
Many of the Old Testament thanksgiving psalms were very likely
written to accompany the offering of material sacrifices in the
Jerusalem Temple. Among the Dead Sea scrolls, one of the most
important documents is known as the *Hodayot* or *Thanksgiving
Hymns*. In these texts the speaker often uses first-person singular
language ("I"). He begins with the words "I thank you, O Lord"
and proceeds to provide the reason why ("for you have . . .").

Some scholars contend that in these first-person singular thanksgivings, we can hear the voice of this Jewish sect's leader, spiritual guide, and hero, who was active in the second century B.C, who was known as the "Teacher of Righteousness."

According to Matthew 11:25-26, Jesus began his thanksgiving in the customary Jewish way: "I thank you, Father, Lord of heaven and earth." His address to God balances the divine immanence ("Father") and the divine transcendence ("Lord of heaven and earth"). The reason for his thanksgiving is the success that Jesus had among the "infants," which is clearly a way of talking about the unlikely and even marginal persons—tax collectors, sinners, prostitutes, and so on—from whom Jesus had received his most positive response (see Matthew 11:19). On the other hand, those who would seem to have been more likely to respond positively to Jesus ("the wise and the intelligent") do not seem to "get" what Jesus was saying. In the context of Matthew's Gospel—and very likely in the context of Jesus' own ministry—it was the Pharisees and the Temple officials who seem especially to have failed to grasp the importance of what Jesus was saying and doing. In his thanksgiving prayer, Jesus attributes this curious situation to God's "gracious will," a term quite frequently used in the Qumran *Thanksgiving Hymns* and other Dead Sea scrolls.

Jesus' thanksgiving prayer is accompanied by his declaration in Matthew 11:27 that as God's Son, he is the revealer and revelation of God and of God's wisdom. And it is accompanied by his invitation in 11:28-30 for those seeking genuine wisdom to come to his school of wisdom where one can find a gentle and humble teacher and rest for one's soul. Compare the similar language used by the Jewish wisdom teacher Jesus ben Sira in describing his own wisdom school in Jerusalem in the early second century B.C. (see Sirach 6:18-31 and 51:23-30).

As we have seen already, prayer is a major theme in Luke's Gospel. It contains not only a sample prayer from Jesus (11:1-4) but also his instructions about persistence in prayer (11:5-13 and 18:1-8) and humility in prayer (18:9-14). Luke's Gospel also portrays Jesus as praying at the most decisive moments in his public ministry. According to Luke 3:21-22, Jesus was praying after his baptism when the Holy Spirit descended upon him and the heavenly voice identified him as God's Son and servant. After his initial successes in healing the sick, Luke tells us that Jesus "would withdraw to deserted places and pray" (5:16). Before choosing the twelve apostles, Jesus is said in Luke 6:12 to have gone out to the mountain to pray and to have "spent the night in prayer to God." In his Sermon on the Plain, he instructs his followers to "bless those who curse you, pray for those who abuse you" (6:28). Prior to Peter's climactic confession of Jesus as "the Messiah of God," Jesus "was praying alone" (9:18). According to Luke 9:29, the transfiguration of Jesus took place "while he was praying." In the passion narrative, Jesus is arrested while he is at prayer on the Mount of Olives (22:39-46). And on the cross he prays for those who were responsible for executing him (23:34) and dies with a prayer (see Psalm 31:5) on his lips: "Father, into your hands I commend my spirit" (Luke 23:46).

The Prayer of God's Son

In comparison with the three synoptic gospels, John's Gospel tells us very little about Jesus' practice of prayer. Only when we reach the farewell discourse in John 14–17 does the topic of prayer come to the fore. In John 14:14 Jesus assures his disciples that prayers in his name will surely be answered: "If in my name you ask me for anything, I will do it." But in 16:26-27, Jesus explains that he has no need to ask the Father on their behalf, since the Father loves them and presumably knows what they need already. There are some echoes here of what has been said about the prayer of petition in the other gospels (see Luke 11:9-13).

What is unique to John's Gospel is Jesus' own very long prayer in John 17. This is the conclusion to his farewell discourse at the Last Supper in John 14–17 and the prelude to the passion narrative that begins in John 18. It is sometimes referred to as Jesus' "high priestly prayer" because in it he performs a "priestly" function by interceding for himself, his disciples, and those who will become disciples through them. But it is better called "the prayer of God's Son," since Jesus prays especially to his heavenly Father in his unique role as the Son of God. Throughout the prayer, Jesus addresses God as "Father" (see 17:1, 5, 11, 21, 24, 25).

Modern scholars often call the farewell discourse in John 14–17 the "testament" of Jesus and associate it with a literary form common in Jewish literature in New Testament times. There are testaments attributed to Abraham, Isaac, Jacob, the twelve sons of Jacob, Moses, Solomon, and Job. A testament contains the last words of the departing hero. In it the hero looks over the past and into the future, and gives advice for those whom he leaves behind on how to behave in the present. Testaments often conclude with the hero's prayer for his children or friends. In his concluding prayer in John 17, Jesus prays in turn for himself (17:1-5), for his disciples (17:6-19), and for those who will come to believe through his disciples (17:20-26).

Jesus' prayer for himself in John 17:1-5 concerns the relationship between his glory and his Father's glory.

¹After Jesus had spoken these words, he looked up to heaven and said, "Father, the hour has come; glorify your Son so that the Son may glorify you, ²since you have given him

authority over all people, to give eternal life to all whom you have given him. ³And this is eternal life, that they may know you, the only true God, and Jesus Christ whom you have sent. ⁴I glorified you on earth by finishing the work that you gave me to do. ⁵So now, Father, glorify me in your own presence with the glory that I had in your presence before the world existed."
(John 17:1-5)

By looking up to heaven and addressing God as "Father," Jesus creates the atmosphere of prayer. He announces that his "hour"— his passion, death, resurrection, and exaltation—has finally come (see John 12:23; 12:27; 13:1; 16:32), and prays that it will be seen for what it really is: a manifestation of God's glory. Just as in carrying out his work of revealing the Father Jesus glorified God, now on the eve of the passion Jesus prays that he may again glorify God and that God may glorify him. He also prays that through his "hour," he may give eternal life to all those whom God has given him. In the "hour" of Jesus, it will become apparent to the eyes of faith that the Father and the Son possess the same divine glory. Thus the readers of John's Gospel are instructed to view what follows in John 18–19 not as a defeat or tragedy but rather as a triumph and an exaltation.

In praying for his disciples in John 17:6-19, Jesus asks that his heavenly Father might protect them, make them holy, and empower them to carry on his mission.

⁶"I have made your name known to those whom you gave me from the world. They were yours, and you gave them to me, and they have kept your word. ⁷Now they know that everything you have given me is from you; ⁸for the

words that you gave to me I have given to them, and they have received them and know in truth that I came from you; and they have believed that you sent me. [9]I am asking on their behalf; I am not asking on behalf of the world, but on behalf of those whom you gave me, because they are yours. [10]All mine are yours, and yours are mine; and I have been glorified in them. [11]And now I am no longer in the world, but they are in the world, and I am coming to you. Holy Father, protect them in your name that you have given me, so that they may be one, as we are one. [12]While I was with them, I protected them in your name that you have given me. I guarded them, and not one of them was lost except the one destined to be lost, so that the scripture might be fulfilled. [13]But now I am coming to you, and I speak these things in the world so that they may have my joy made complete in themselves. [14]I have given them your word, and the world has hated them because they do not belong to the world, just as I do not belong to the world. [15]I am not asking you to take them out of the world, but I ask you to protect them from the evil one. [16]They do not belong to the world, just as I do not belong to the world. [17]Sanctify them in the truth; your word is truth. [18]As you have sent me into the world, so I have sent them into the world. [19]And for their sakes I sanctify myself, so that they also may be sanctified in truth."
(John 17:6-19)

Before making his prayer in John 17:9, Jesus describes his disciples as the ones to whom he has revealed God and manifested God's glory. They in turn have accepted Jesus' words and recognized that he has come from God. In his prayer, Jesus distinguishes them from "the world," taken in its negative Johannine sense as the forces of evil arrayed against God and his Son. The disciples have been taken into the relationship that exists between the Father and the Son. The departing Jesus prays that they may continue in this relationship and that God will protect them from "the evil one." But that relationship is not purely defensive or protective. Rather, Jesus also prays that they will carry on his mission for which he had been sent into the world (17:18) and that they will be swept up into the holiness and truth of God (17:17, 19). The fragility of the disciples' situation is underscored by the repeated references to the opposition that they will face from "the world" (17:9, 11, 13, 14, 15, 16, 18).

Finally, in John 17:20-26 Jesus prays for those who will come to believe in him through his disciples.

> [20]"I ask not only on behalf of these, but also on behalf of those who will believe in me through their word, [21]that they may all be one. As you, Father, are in me and I am in you, may they also be in us, so that the world may believe that you have sent me. [22]The glory that you have given me I have given them, so that they may be one, as we are one, [23]I in them and you in me, that they may become completely one, so that the world may know that you have sent me and have loved them even as you have loved me. [24]Father, I desire that those also, whom you have given me, may be with me where I am, to see my glory, which you have given me because you loved me before the foundation of the world.
> [25] "Righteous Father, the world does not know you, but I know you; and these know that you have sent me. [26]I made your name known to them, and I will make it known, so

that the love with which you have loved me may be in them,
and I in them."
(John 17:20-26)

The same points are made in both John 17:21 and 17:22-23.
Jesus prays that all these persons may be one as he and the Father
are one so that they may share in the divine unity and that they
may come to believe that God sent the Son. The parallelism is
broken at the end of 17:23 with the notice that the Father loves
them "even as you [the Father] have loved me," which prepares
for Jesus' wish at the end of the prayer that the Father's love "may
be in them, and I in them" (17:26). The object of the church's mission is "the world," now understood more positively or at least
neutrally. Caught up in the mystery of love between the Father
and the Son that existed before the creation of the world (17:24),
these believers will share in the divine glory, divine unity, and
divine mission. The Son of God prays that his disciples and those
who come to believe through them may enjoy the same relationship with the Father that he himself experiences. The Son of God
prays that they too may be children of God.

BRINGING THE CONTEXTS TOGETHER

There is a profound theology of prayer in Judaism that has
become part of the Christian tradition of prayer through Jesus
and the early Christians. It is the framework within which we ourselves can and should pray today. As "our Father in heaven," the
God to whom we pray is both immanent ("our Father") and tran-
scendent ("in heaven"). This God can be addressed directly as the
Father of our Lord Jesus Christ, and not only hears our prayers
but also wants to respond positively to them. At the same time,

this God is the Lord of all creation, the one who creates and sustains us and yet remains infinitely superior to us.

As mediated through Jesus and the early Christians, the Jewish prayer tradition has given us the language and the literary forms of prayer that most of us use in our prayer today. Moreover, the words and forms of our formal liturgies have been shaped by the psalms and other biblical and early Jewish conventions. From this tradition we can also learn the value of pious flexibility even in our formal prayers, and we can come to appreciate better the creative relationship between personal prayer and communal prayer.

In the Lord's Prayer that Jesus has taught us to pray, the central theme is the kingdom of God. This was also the central theme of Jesus' parables and other teachings about prayer and other topics. Even his miracles were not so much spectacular displays of his personal power as they were signs pointing to the presence and future fullness of God's reign. His insistence on boldness and persistence in prayer should inspire us to be less passive and guarded in our prayers. His example of praying at the decisive moments in his life is surely worthy of imitation on our part. And finally, as his farewell prayer in John 17 suggests, we now have the risen Jesus praying and interceding for us with his heavenly Father.

Think, Pray, and Act

Consider how the prayers of Jesus and his teachings on prayer in the gospels might enrich your appreciation of Jesus and your own way of praying.

Think
🎵 When you say the Lord's Prayer, how do you imagine God?

What do you want God to do? Where do you fit in?

§ How strongly do you believe in the prayer of petition? Are you just covering your bets? Or is there some experience that has confirmed your belief in the power of prayer?

§ For what have you asked God recently? Did you get what you asked for?

Pray
§ Recite the Lord's Prayer slowly and thoughtfully. Do you understand it as a prayer for the full coming of God's kingdom?

§ Place yourself in God's presence, and ask God for the three things you want most.

Act
§ Set some time apart to pray for others and their needs.

§ Is there anyone whom you need to forgive before seeking forgiveness from God? How might you go about doing so?

Chapter Three

Jesus' Laments in the Passion Narratives

The traditional devotion known as the Seven Last Words of Jesus is often part of Good Friday observances in Catholic parishes. Stretched out over three hours or so, it can be a powerful and spiritually fruitful way of entering into the mystery of Jesus' passion and death. Most of these seven "words" are deeply rooted in the biblical tradition of the lament psalms, by far the largest category among the 150 prayers gathered in the Old Testament Book of Psalms. Indeed, it is possible to view Jesus in the Garden of Gethsemane and on the cross at Calvary as the incarnation of the biblical lament psalms.

JESUS' PRAYER IN GETHSEMANE

In the gospel passion narratives, the episode of Jesus in Gethsemane serves as the bridge between his Last Supper and his betrayal by Judas and arrest. "Gethsemane," which means "oil press," was a plot of land on the Mount of Olives, east of the walled city of Jerusalem. According to all four gospels, Jesus went there with his disciples after the Last Supper. Since Passover was a pilgrimage feast and drew large crowds to Jerusalem, we should not imagine the area to have been totally deserted. The fact that Judas had to devise a kiss as a signal to identify Jesus so that the soldiers might arrest the right man indicates that there were many others in the area, with some probably camping out for the evening.

Jesus' purpose in going to Gethsemane was to pray, and in particular to gather his thoughts and emotions, and to focus on the events before him—his arrest, trials, scourging, crucifixion, and death.

> [32]They went to a place called Gethsemane; and he said to his disciples, "Sit here while I pray." [33]He took with him Peter and James and John, and began to be distressed and agitated. [34]And said to them, "I am deeply grieved, even to death; remain here, and keep awake." [35]And going a little farther, he threw himself on the ground and prayed that, if it were possible, the hour might pass from him. [36]He said, "Abba, Father, for you all things are possible; remove this cup from me; yet, not what I want, but what you want." [37]He came and found them sleeping; and he said to Peter, "Simon, are you asleep? Could you not keep awake one hour? [38]Keep awake and pray that you may not come into the time of trial; the spirit indeed is willing, but the flesh is weak." [39]And again he went away and prayed, saying the same words. [40]And once more he came and found them sleeping, for their eyes were very heavy; and they did not know what to say to him. [41]He came a third time and said to them, "Are you still sleeping and taking your rest? Enough! The hour has come; the Son of Man is betrayed into the hands of sinners. [42]Get up, let us be going. See, my betrayer is at hand."
> (Mark 14:32-42)

Finding a relatively isolated place, he summoned the three disciples—Peter, James, and John, who constituted the inner core among his followers—to accompany him and to keep watch while he prayed. According to Mark 14:32-42 (see Matthew 26:36-46; Luke 22:39-46; John 18:1), Jesus engaged in three rounds of prayer, and each time at the end he found his disciples asleep. Finally recognizing the inevitability of his arrest and the events that would follow, Jesus goes forward to meet his fate and says, "Get up, let us be going. See, my betrayer is at hand" (Mark 14:42).

Mark records two sayings spoken by Jesus that can count as prayers in this episode. One, in 14:34, is an allusion to Psalms 42 and 43, and the other, in 14:36, is a direct address to his heavenly Father. In 14:33 Mark describes Jesus as being in a highly emotional state of distress and agitation, and then in 14:34 records his words to his disciples, "I am deeply grieved, even to death." The description and the direct statement are generally regarded as alluding to what serves as a refrain in Psalms 42 and 43, "My soul is cast down within me" (42:5) and "Why are you cast down, O my soul?" 42:11; 43:5). The allusion is somewhat obscured in the NRSV translation. A more literal translation of the Greek texts of Mark 14:34 ("my soul is sorrowful") and of Psalm 42:5 ("Why are you sorrowful, O my soul") brings out the allusion more clearly. Thus Jesus, the innocent sufferer, makes his own the language of the biblical lament psalms.

The laments constitute the largest literary category of psalms in the biblical Book of Psalms. (For examples, see Psalms 3, 5, 6, 7, 13, 17, 22, 26, 27, and 28.) The laments address God directly and usually contain a description of the present suffering, an affirmation of trust and hope in God, a plea for God to act on the speaker's behalf, and a final note of thanksgiving (as if God had already acted). The most famous lament is Psalm 22 (see the next section).

Throughout Jewish and Christian history, the biblical laments, with their open and metaphorical language, have provided words and images for those who are suffering. These psalms have enabled people to express both their pain and their faith and hope in God and so overcome the isolation and hopelessness that often accompany suffering. One early Christian approach to reading the psalms was to interpret them as "the Book of Christ," as if Jesus was the speaker of all the psalms, and of the laments in particular.

It is generally agreed that what are now known as Psalms 42 and 43 originally constituted a single lament psalm. It contains complaints (42:3, 9); professions of faith (42:2, 5-6, 11; 43:5); a petition for divine help (42:11); and a reference to a thanksgiving sacrifice (43:4). The allusion to Psalms 42–43 early in the Markan passion narrative suggests a powerful connection between the biblical laments and Jesus as the man of sorrows. This connection will reach its climax in Jesus' last words from the cross in Mark 15:34 ("My God, my God, why have you forsaken me?"), which are the first words of Psalm 22.

The prayer of Jesus in Gethsemane is quoted in Mark 14:36: "Abba, Father, for you all things are possible; remove this cup from me; yet, not what I want, but what you want." The introduction to the prayer in 14:35 captures the emotional distress that Jesus was experiencing ("he threw himself on the ground") and summarizes the content of the prayer ("that the hour might pass from him").

The address in Jesus' prayer combines the Aramaic (*Abba*) and Greek (*Pater*) words for "Father." The word *Abba* is generally regarded as Jesus' own characteristic way of addressing God in prayer. Its use among early Christians is seen in Romans 8:15 and Galatians 4:6. The declaration that "all things are possible" with God echoes Jesus' own statement in Mark 10:27 and counters any misunderstanding about Jesus' lack of faith in God. The "cup" is synonymous with "the hour" in 14:35. In the Old Testament, the "cup" image was often used by the prophets to describe the suffering that God will bring upon Israel's enemies or upon Israel itself (see Isaiah 51:17; Jeremiah 25:15-16; 51:7; Ezekiel 23:33; Psalm 75:8). In Mark's Gospel the image of the cup is associated with Jesus' own suffering in 10:38-39 ("the cup which I drink you will drink") and in 14:24-25 ("this is my blood of the covenant, which is poured out for many"). Thus, when we share the cup at the Eucharist, we are entering into the suffering and death of Jesus. After expressing his personal struggle, Jesus accepts the cup of suffering as being in accord with God's will ("not what I want, but what you want"). His words echo the petition of the Lord's Prayer in Matthew 6:10 ("your will be done") and express Jesus' perfect acceptance of God's will.

Besides the address to God as "Abba, Father" and Jesus' acceptance of God's "will," there is perhaps a further allusion to the Lord's Prayer in Jesus' warning to the disciples to "pray that you may not come into the time of trial" (Mark 14:38). While Mark never provides the full text of the Lord's Prayer (as in Matthew 6:9-13 and Luke 11:2-4), these parallels or allusions suggest that he knew it. Since the Lord's Prayer is the prayer for the full coming of God's kingdom ("Thy kingdom come"), these echoes contribute to the eschatological dimension of the passion narrative. That is, Jesus' suffering, death, and resurrection are pivotal to the full coming of God's kingdom. These echoes also help us to make connections between Jesus as he moves toward the cross and the language we use in what has become the Christian prayer *par excellence*.

Jesus' prayer in Gethsemane reminds us that Jesus had to school himself to accept the suffering that awaited him. In doing so, he placed himself in the tradition of the biblical lament psalms. He called upon God as his Father, expressed his trust in God's power, evoked the cup as the biblical image of suffering, and resolved his mixed feelings by submitting to God's will and to the mystery of the cross. When we recite the Lord's Prayer and share the eucharistic cup, we place ourselves beside Jesus and enter more deeply into his passion and death.

JESUS' LAST WORDS ACCORDING TO MARK AND MATTHEW

According to Mark 15:34 (and Matthew 27:46), Jesus shortly before his death on the cross cried out, "My God, my God, why have you forsaken me?" These are also the first words in Psalm 22, which is one of the most elaborate examples of the lament category in the biblical Book of Psalms. It is important to read Jesus' last words according to Mark and Matthew in the context of both the New Testament passion narratives and the whole text of Psalm 22.

[33]When it was noon, darkness came over the whole land until three in the afternoon. [34]At three o'clock Jesus cried out with a loud voice, "Eloi, Eloi, lema sabachthani?" which means, "My God, my God, why have you forsaken me?" [35]When some of the bystanders heard it, they said, "Listen, he is calling for Elijah." [36]And someone ran, filled a sponge with sour wine, put it on a stick, and gave it to him to drink, saying, "Wait, let us see whether Elijah will come to take him down." [37]Then Jesus gave a loud cry and breathed his last. [38]And the curtain of the temple was torn in two, from top to bottom. [39]Now when the centurion, who stood fac-

ing him, saw that in this way he breathed his last, he said, "Truly this man was God's Son!"

⁴⁰There were also women looking on from a distance; among them were Mary Magdalene, and Mary the mother of James the younger and of Joses, and Salome. ⁴¹These used to follow him and provided for him when he was in Galilee; and there were many other women who had come up with him to Jerusalem.
(Mark 15:33-41)

The account of Jesus' death in Mark 15:33-41, while written in a spare and objective style, is a rich mixture of cosmic and earthly portents, a report about Jesus' last words and his death, and reactions from bystanders. After recounting the portent of darkness from noon to 3:00 p.m., Mark tells us that Jesus cried out in Aramaic the first words of Psalm 22. Then there is confusion about whether Jesus was calling for Elijah, and someone offers him vinegary wine. The death of Jesus is marked by his loud shout, for which no content is given, and his last breath ("he gave up his spirit"). At the moment of Jesus' death, the veil in the sanctuary of the Jerusalem Temple is ripped in two. The narrative ends with a climactic reaction by the Roman centurion overseeing Jesus' execution ("Truly this man was God's Son!") and a notice that several of Jesus' women followers had witnessed his death at a distance.

While this passage is full of fascinating and meaningful details, here I want only to focus on what Mark presents as the last words of Jesus, which are also the first words of Psalm 22. In the context of the whole of Mark's Gospel, interpreting these words ("My God, my God, why have you forsaken me?") as a cry of utter despair on Jesus' part makes no sense. Throughout his narrative,

Mark has portrayed Jesus as a wise teacher, a powerful miracle worker, and a noble figure who relied totally on God as his heavenly Father. To suggest that Jesus threw all this aside at the moment of his death would make nonsense out of the rest of his gospel. Would anyone have written a gospel (which means "good news") about a tragic figure whose life ended in total despair? What would be the good news there?

It is possible that on the historical level, Jesus did feel abandoned in his final hour. His closest followers, apart from a few women, had fled in fear. And he was opposed by powerful groups within his own people, including the chief priests, the elders, and the Pharisees, and by the Roman authorities. He may possibly have imagined momentarily that even his heavenly Father had abandoned him in the midst of his intense suffering. But that is at best speculation. A literary and theological approach to Mark 15:34, however, correctly places more emphasis on reading Psalm 22 as a prayer on the lips of the dying Jesus. This is entirely coherent with the tradition of the biblical laments and Psalm 22 in particular.

> [1]My God, my God, why have you forsaken me?
>> Why are you so far from helping me, from the words of my groaning?
> [2]O my God, I cry by day, but you do not answer;
>> and by night, but find no rest.
>
> [3]Yet you are holy,
>> enthroned on the praises of Israel.
> [4]In you our ancestors trusted;
>> they trusted, and you delivered them.
> [5]To you they cried, and were saved;
>> in you they trusted, and were not put to shame.

⁶But I am a worm, and not human;
  scorned by others, and despised by the people.
⁷All who see me mock at me;
  they make mouths at me, they shake their heads;
⁸"Commit your cause to the LORD; let him deliver—
  let him rescue the one in whom he delights!"

⁹Yet it was you who took me from the womb;
  you kept me safe on my mother's breast.
¹⁰On you I was cast from my birth,
  and since my mother bore me you have been my God.
¹¹Do not be far from me,
    for trouble is near
    and there is no one to help.

¹²Many bulls encircle me,
  strong bulls of Bashan surround me;
¹³they open wide their mouths at me,
  like a ravening and roaring lion.

¹⁴I am poured out like water,
  and all my bones are out of joint;
my heart is like wax;
  it is melted within my breast;
¹⁵my mouth is dried up like a potsherd,
  and my tongue sticks to my jaws;
  you lay me in the dust of death.

¹⁶For dogs are all around me;
  a company of evildoers encircles me.
My hands and feet have shriveled;

¹⁷I can count all my bones.
They stare and gloat over me;
¹⁸they divide my clothes among themselves,
     and for my clothing they cast lots.

¹⁹But you, O Lord, do not be far away!
     O my help, come quickly to my aid!
²⁰Deliver my soul from the sword,
     my life from the power of the dog!
          ²¹Save me from the mouth of the lion!

From the horns of the wild oxen you have rescued me.
²²I will tell of your name to my brothers and sisters;
     in the midst of the congregation I will praise you:
²³You who fear the Lord, praise him!
     All you offspring of Jacob, glorify him;
     stand in awe of him, all you offspring of Israel!
²⁴For he did not despise or abhor
     the affliction of the afflicted;
he did not hide his face from me,
     but heard when I cried to him.

²⁵From you comes my praise in the great congregation;
     my vows I will pay before those who fear him.
²⁶The poor shall eat and be satisfied;
     those who seek him shall praise the Lord.
     May your hearts live forever!
²⁷All the ends of the earth shall remember
     and turn to the Lord;
and all the families of the nations
     shall worship before him.

²⁸For dominion belongs to the LORD,
   and he rules over the nations.

²⁹To him, indeed, shall all who sleep in the earth bow
      down;
   before him shall bow all who go down to the dust,
   and I shall live for him.
³⁰Posterity will serve him;
   future generations will be told about the Lord,
³¹and proclaim his deliverance to a people yet unborn,
   saying that he has done it.
(Psalm 22)

In the preceding passage (Mark 15:21-32), there were already allusions to Psalm 22 in the dividing of Jesus' garments (Mark 15:24 = Psalm 22:18), and in the bystanders mocking and shaking their heads at Jesus (Mark 15:29-32 = Psalm 22:7). Indeed, when the early Christians came to tell the story of Jesus' death, they cast it to a large extent in terms found in the Suffering Servant Song in Isaiah 53 and in the Psalm of the Righteous Sufferer, Psalm 22. They regarded Jesus as the one who had fulfilled those prophecies. The language of the immediate context for Jesus' last words, according to Mark (and Matthew), prepares us to interpret them in the context of Psalm 22 taken as a whole. That is, we should regard them not as a cry of personal despair but rather as a prayer for divine help in the midst of intense suffering and a proclamation of divine vindication and perhaps even of resurrection.

Psalm 22 follows the script of the biblical laments. It begins with a direct address to God ("My God, my God"). What follows in 22:1-11 is an alternation of complaints (verses 1-2, 6-8) and expressions of trust in God (verses 3-5, 9-11). The complaints are quite vivid ("you do not answer" . . . "I am a worm, and not human"). In emphasizing the importance of Psalm 22 for under-standing Jesus' last words in Mark 15:34, I am not suggesting that Jesus is playacting. His sufferings were certainly real. My point, rather, is that here as in the episode in Gethsemane, Jesus is the personification or incarnation of the biblical lament psalms. At the same time, the psalmist's expressions of trust appeal first to what God had done for his people Israel in the exodus ("you delivered them") and in his own personal life ("You kept me safe on my mother's breast").

The mix of complaint and profession of trust yields in Psalm 22:12-18 to an extended lamentation that alternates between threats from fierce animals (verses 12–13, 16a) and self-descrip-tions of great suffering (verses 14–15, 16b-18). The images of bulls, lions, and dogs all emphasize the objective physical dan-gers surrounding the psalmist. The "I" statements express the subjective terrors that the psalmist endured in all the various parts of his body. The petition proper in 22:19-21a ("O Lord, do not be far away") continues the animal imagery with refer-ence to being saved from "the power of the dog" and "the mouth of the lion."

While the quotation of Psalm 22:1 and the echoes of Psalm 22:1-21 elsewhere in Mark's passion narrative identify Jesus with the speakers in the Old Testament laments, it is important to read the whole psalm. Many of the lament psalms end with a brief statement about a thanksgiving sacrifice having been offered or promised. Psalm 22 contains this element presented in elabo-rate detail in verses 21b-31. Continuing the animal imagery, the psalmist proclaims, "From the horns of the wild oxen you have rescued me." Then he promises to proclaim what God has done on his behalf "in the midst of the congregation," which is the biblical concept of thanksgiving, as we have seen. Thanksgiving sacrifices at the Jerusalem Temple were often accompanied by a festive meal, and so the psalmist promises that "the poor shall eat and be satisfied." Beyond his family and friends as well as "the poor," the psalmist goes on to invite "all the ends of the earth" to join in celebrating his good fortune. That includes all the living ("all the families of the nations"), the dead ("all who sleep in the earth"), and even those who are yet to be born ("a people yet unborn").

While the NRSV translation of Psalm 22:29 is probably clearer than the Hebrew original allows, there may well be a reference to resurrection there: "To him [the LORD], indeed, shall all who sleep in the earth bow down; / before him [the LORD] shall bow all who go down to the dust, and I shall live for him." The Greek text (Psalm 21:30b LXX) supports this kind of reading: "Before him [the LORD] all those who descend into the earth will bow down, and my soul shall live for him." Though there are translation problems, this verse can be interpreted as hinting at and supporting early Jewish belief in the resurrection of the dead.

When we read the second part of Psalm 22 with Jesus in mind and even as the speaker, then this psalm serves as a witness not only of the suffering of Jesus but also to the vindication of Jesus in his resurrection from the dead. In other words, the psalm makes us look beyond Jesus' passion and death to the empty tomb and the young man's proclamation that "he has been raised; he is not here" (Mark 16:6). Far from being a cry of despair, the words "My God, my God, why have you forsaken me?" on the lips of the dying Jesus place him in solidarity with all suffering persons on Good Friday. And it reminds us that he has been vindicated by his heavenly Father in his resurrection on Easter Sunday.

Jesus' Last Words according to Luke and John

Luke's passion narrative adds three sayings to the corpus of Jesus' last words. In each case Jesus shows himself to be faithful to the principles that he taught and exemplified in his own public ministry. With his prayer "Father, forgive them; for they do not know what they are doing" (Luke 23:34), Jesus shows himself to be faithful to his principle of love of enemies (see 6:27-36) and to his teaching about forgiveness (11:4). In his promise to the "good thief" in 23:43 ("today you will be with me in Paradise"), he continues his ministry to marginal persons ("tax collectors and sinners") even while he is dying on the cross. And in expressing his trust in God to the end in 23:46 ("Father, into your hands I commend my spirit"), Jesus exemplifies his own insistence on trusting in God's compassionate care (12:22-34).

In the third of these last sayings according to Luke, Jesus makes his own the words of Psalm 31:5 when he says, "Father, into your hands I commend my spirit." Psalm 31 is a lament in which the speaker addresses God directly ("O LORD"), describes the present suffering with great emotion, professes trust in God's care, and asks God to do something to relieve the suffering. It ends as do most laments with words of thanksgiving, either anticipating God's action in the future or bearing witness to it as if it had already taken place. What is especially important about this psalm is its expressions of trust in God in 31:5 ("into your hand I commit my spirit") and in 31:14-15 ("But I trust in you, O LORD; I say, 'You are my God.' My times are in your hand").

Psalm 31 is the prayer of an innocent sufferer, the victim of plotting by his enemies. Likewise, according to Luke and the other Evangelists, Jesus is an innocent sufferer, the victim of trumped-up charges, lying witnesses, and corrupt officials. Thus, the psalmist and Jesus stand in solidarity with other innocent sufferers in the past, present, and future. Throughout Luke's account of his public ministry, Jesus prays at all the most important moments. His death on the cross is the most important moment of all. Here Jesus makes his own, personifies, and incarnates the spirituality of the biblical laments, and provides a good example of fidelity to all who suffer.

The final words of Jesus in John's Gospel are more statements than prayers. But they do allude to Scripture and to prayer. According to John 19:26-27, Jesus commends his mother to the Beloved Disciple ("Woman, here is your son"), and the Beloved Disciple to his mother ("Here is your mother"). At the cross they all constitute a community of compassion and suffering. Jesus shows himself concerned especially for the continuation of the new family of faith that he had founded. In John 19:28 Scripture is said to be fulfilled with Jesus' cry, "I am thirsty." The reference is likely to Psalm 22:15 ("my mouth is dried up like a potsherd, / and my tongue sticks to my jaw") and/or to Psalm 69:21 ("for my thirst they gave me vinegar to drink"). Both are lament psalms.

According to John's chronology, Jesus died in the late afternoon of Good Friday, when the Passover lambs were being sacrificed in the Jerusalem Temple. His last word in John 19:30 is translated as "It is finished." But the Greek word *tetelestai* conveys more than simply the end of a life in death. The root *telos* can refer not only to an endpoint in time but also to a goal having been reached or a purpose having been carried out or achieved. In the Johannine context, it suggests the nuances of the Son's fulfilling God's will as expressed in the Scriptures and his carrying out perfectly the role of "the Lamb of God who takes away the sin of the world" (John 1:29). The phrase "[he] gave up his spirit" at the end of 19:30 can be taken to describe Jesus' death (giving up his last breath) and/or his bestowal of the Holy Spirit at the moment of death (see 7:39 and 20:22).

Bringing the Contexts Together

The biblical lament psalms are important resources when we find ourselves in the midst of suffering. Most obviously there are many of them—about one-third of the collection that is the Book of Psalms. They remind us that even though in our suffering we may feel isolated and abandoned, we stand in community and solidarity with sufferers over the span of many centuries. Also, they provide us with the words and images that as suffering persons we may need in order to express our own pain. Moreover, they allow us to take off the religious censor and address hard questions to God: Why am I suffering? Where are you in the midst of my suffering? When and how will it end? Finally the lament psalms usually end with a word of hope, thus reassuring us that suffering does not always have the last word.

While the Evangelists do refer often to the physical sufferings of Jesus, they give even more attention to the misunderstanding and rejection that marked Jesus' public ministry and eventually led to his death on the cross. Even his own disciples deserted him in the end. Nevertheless, Jesus drew his courage and spiritual sustenance from his intimate relationship with his heavenly Father (*Abba*), and so was able to come to accept the cup of suffering as being in accord with his Father's will. While he makes his own the lamentations expressed so vividly in Psalm 22, we can and should also look to his resurrection as God's final vindication of his beloved Son.

Think, Pray, and Act

Consider how the biblical laments and the last words of Jesus might enrich your appreciation of Jesus and your own way of praying.

Think

✤ When suffering comes to you, what are your first reactions? Is it "What have I done wrong?" or "Why me?" or something else?

✤ How might the Old Testament lament psalms help you to put your suffering into perspective, and achieve some peace of soul?

✤ When you participate in the Eucharist, do you connect your reception of the sacred elements with the passion and death of Jesus and with the sufferings of people all over the world?

Pray

✤ Reread the whole text of Psalm 22 slowly and meditatively, and give special attention to its parallels with Jesus' passion, death, and resurrection.

✤ With reference to whatever sufferings there may be in your life at present, ask God to help you drink the cup of suffering and accept them as God's will.

Act

✤ Is there something you might do to alleviate the suffering of someone else in your everyday life? Who? How? When?

Chapter Four

Early Hymns and Creeds
about Christ

J esus' death on the cross was by no means the end of his story. On Easter Sunday his tomb was found to be empty, a fact quickly interpreted to mean that he had been miraculously raised from the dead. This belief was reinforced by a series of appearances of the risen Jesus to followers who knew that he had died and nevertheless experienced him as alive again. This conviction in turn led to the revitalization of the Jesus movement and produced various expressions of belief about Jesus in hymns and credal statements.

In the early second century A.D., Pliny, the Roman governor of Bithynia in north-central Asia Minor, now modern Turkey, reported to the Roman emperor Trajan that the Christians there "were in the habit of meeting on a certain fixed day before it was light, when they sang in alternative verses a hymn to Christ as to a god" (*Letters* 10.96). While we do not know exactly which hymns they sang, the prayers and creeds treated in this chapter may have been among them. They are eloquent witnesses to what early Christians believed and taught about Jesus. Bear in mind always that most of these texts reflect the development of beliefs about Jesus that arose between Jesus' death in A.D. 30 and the earliest Pauline letters in A.D. 50.

JESUS CHRIST AS THE SERVANT OF GOD
(PHILIPPIANS 2:6-11)

According to Acts 16:11-40, Paul came to Philippi in northern Greece and founded his first Christian community in Europe in that city. His initial success was due in large part to Lydia and other women who lived in Philippi. Paul wrote his letter in the mid-50s of the first century to the Philippians from prison, probably at Ephesus, as a way of extending his pastoral care for them and dealing with certain problems that had arisen there after his departure. They are often described as his favorite community. In writing to the Philippians, Paul wanted to reassure them about his situation in prison and to urge them to greater mutual respect and unity in light of tensions within the community. He also warned them against the claims of rival Jewish Christian missionaries and thanked them for a generous gift that they had sent to him during his imprisonment. The most famous passage in this letter is Philippians 2:6-11.

It is widely held that Paul sought to resolve the disunity and tensions within the Christian community at Philippi by quoting an early Christian hymn about the humiliation and the exaltation of Christ, the Servant of God. That the passage represents the quotation of existing material is indicated by its somewhat awkward fit in its present context and its peculiar vocabulary ("the form of God," "equality with God," "something to be exploited," and so on.) That it was a hymn or part of a hymn is suggested by its use of parallelism and rhythmic speech. It is possible, though unlikely, that Paul composed the hymn or wrote here in a particularly hymnic or poetic style. It more likely arose as a hymn in the context of early Christian worship. And so it can tell us something about very early Christian beliefs regarding Jesus. Paul's letter was composed in the mid-50s of the first century, so the hymn must have been older than that. The original language of the hymn may have been Aramaic, since the present Greek text can be translated back into Aramaic fairly easily. Thus, the theological language and concepts of Philippians 2:6-11 are very important for understanding first-generation Christian beliefs about Jesus.

The hymn is introduced in Philippians 2:5 by a plea for the Philippians to have "the same mind" as Christ had. The idea is that they should make their own the attitude of humility and selflessness shown by Christ in his incarnation and death on the cross.

> [6]who, though he was in the form of God,
>   did not regard equality with God
>   as something to be exploited,
> [7]but emptied himself,
>   taking the form of a slave,
>   being born in human likeness.
> And being found in human form,
>   [8]he humbled himself
>   and became obedient to the point of death—
>   even death on a cross.
>
> [9]Therefore God also highly exalted him
>   and gave him the name
>   that is above every name,
> [10]so that at the name of Jesus
>   every knee should bend,
>   in heaven and on earth and under the earth,
> [11]and every tongue should confess

that Jesus Christ is Lord,
to the glory of God the Father.
(Philippians 2:6-11)

Various structural outlines of the hymn have been proposed. The most popular outline distinguishes two stanzas of three verses each: the humiliation of Christ (2:6-8), and the exaltation of Christ (2:9-11). The first stanza describes Christ as equal to or like God (2:6), his incarnation (2:7), and his death (2:8). Some interpreters regard "even death on a cross" at the end of 2:8 as an addition by Paul or another editor. The second stanza deals with the exaltation of Christ as Lord (2:9) and the homage paid to him by all creation (2:10-11). Another outline discerns three stanzas of four lines each: Christ the perfect image of God (2:6-7b), Christ humbling himself and accepting death (2:7c-8), and the exaltation of Christ as Lord (2:9-11).

The content of this early Christian hymn deserves to be taken very seriously. The claim that Christ was "in the form of God" (2:6) refers to his form or condition, which points to his essential status or character. In other words, he enjoyed divine status. Though some interpreters find an allusion here to Adam (Genesis 1:26-27), the expression is better taken as a description of Christ's divinity in terms of his preexistence (see Colossians 1:15-20; John 1:1-18; Hebrews 1:3).

During his earthly life, Christ did not seek to be treated on a par with God. In other words, he refused to exploit his divine status for his own advantage. But when he "emptied himself" (Philippians 2:7), he did not cease to be divine. Rather, he gave up the "form" of God and took up the form of "slave" or "servant" in becoming human. And in becoming human and even accepting death on the cross (2:8), Jesus proved himself to be the perfect example of humility and obedience to God, an example that his followers should imitate (see 2:5).

The first part of the hymn brings to mind the figure of the "Servant of the Lord" in Isaiah 40–55, especially the two passages (50:4-9 and 52:13–53:12) where the Servant's sufferings are described in graphic terms. According to Isaiah 50:6, the Servant's back was beaten, his beard was pulled, and he was insulted and spat upon. According to 52:14, he suffered so much abuse that his appearance was marred "beyond human semblance." What is most striking about the Servant's sufferings as they are interpreted in Isaiah 53 is the insistence on their vicarious or expiatory value: "he was wounded for our transgressions" (53:5); "the LORD laid on him the iniquity of us all" (53:6); and "he bore the sin of many, and made intercession for the transgressors" (53:12).

The Servant songs and all of Isaiah 40–55 reflect the experience of the Jewish exiled community in Babylon in the early sixth century B.C. and the permission granted by the Persian king Cyrus the Great in 539 B.C. for them to return to Jerusalem and to rebuild their Temple there. The prophet used the figure of the Servant of the Lord to help explain the massive suffering that Israel had endured when the city and the Temple were destroyed and their political and religious leaders were exiled to Babylon.

Who was the Servant? Some scholars regard the Servant as a collective symbolic representation of the exiled community or of Israel as a whole. Others argue for identifying the Servant as a specific individual—the prophet himself, a leader in the exile community, a legitimate claimant to the royal throne of Judah, or someone else.

There is no real clarity or consensus about the identity of the Servant figure described by the sixth-century prophet. However, at a very early moment in their movement's history, early

Christians became convinced that the one who best fits the profile of the Servant of the Lord was Jesus of Nazareth. The most explicit identification occurs in Acts 8:26-40, when the evangelist Philip explains to the Ethiopian eunuch that the person about whom he had been reading in Isaiah 53 was Jesus. Throughout the gospels, Jesus is described in terms used in Isaiah 40–55 with regard to the Servant: the light of the nations, the Lamb of God, the one with whom God is pleased, and so forth. The figure of the Servant in Isaiah 40–55 helps to provide the biblical context for the assertion in the early Christian hymn that Christ "emptied himself, taking the form of a slave [or, servant]" and "humbled himself and became obedient to the point of death—even death on a cross."

In the second stanza (Philippians 2:9-11), the resurrection of Jesus is taken as a part or moment in the larger process of God's exaltation of Jesus. The "name that is above every name" presumably is "Lord" (*Kyrios* in Greek), the title applied to the God of Israel in the Greek version of the Old Testament. Here the hymn helps to explain how the title "Lord" could be applied to Jesus in early Christian circles without destroying Jewish and Christian beliefs in the one and only God. The assertion is that God gave the name Lord/*Kyrios* to Jesus at his resurrection/exaltation. Because the name of Jesus Christ is now connected with the Lord (see 2:9, 11), all creatures in the universe ought to pay him homage.

The hymn reaches its theological climax in Philippians 2:11 with a reference to an already existing summary of Christian faith: "Jesus Christ is Lord" (see Romans 10:9; 1 Corinthians 12:3). In fact, this summary may have been the starting point of the hymn, which explains why and how Jesus can be celebrated as Lord. The final phrase "to the glory of God the Father" clarifies the goal or purpose of the entire process described in the hymn.

The ultimate purpose of Christ's humiliation and exaltation was the proclamation and acknowledgment of the glory of God (see 1 Corinthians 15:28).

Jesus Christ as the Wisdom of God
(Colossians 1:15-20)

Colossae was a city in western Asia Minor about a hundred miles east of Ephesus. The Christian community there was founded not by Paul directly but rather by one of Paul's co-workers, Epaphras, who was also known as Epaphroditus (see Colossians 1:7-8). The letter appears to have been written by Paul while he was in prison (4:3) in the mid-50s, perhaps at Ephesus. More likely, however, it was composed in Paul's name by a co-worker or admirer at a somewhat later date, around A.D. 80. In either case, it is best interpreted as a warning directed mainly to Gentile Christians against the attractions of an esoteric Judaism that may have appropriated some elements from Greek philosophy and mystery religions (see 2:8-23). In this context, what seems to have been an early Christian hymn about Jesus Christ as the Wisdom of God in 1:15-20 provides the theological foundation for the writer's presentation about the absolute sufficiency of Christ's death and resurrection to bring about salvation and true enlightenment.

> [15]He is the image of the invisible God, the firstborn of all creation; [16]for in him all things in heaven and on earth were created, things visible and invisible, whether thrones or dominions or rulers or powers—all things have been created through him and for him. [17]He himself is before all

things, and in him all things hold together. [18]He is the head
of the body, the church; he is the beginning, the firstborn
from the dead, so that he might come to have first place in
everything. [19]For in him all the fullness of God was pleased
to dwell, [20]and through him God was pleased to reconcile
to himself all things, whether on earth or in heaven, by
making peace through the blood of his cross.
(Colossians 1:15-20)

The hymn may have been introduced by a blessing ("Blessed be
our Lord Jesus Christ . . .") to which the two main sections were
attached. The two main parts of the hymn concern the role of
Christ as first in the order of creation (Colossians 1:15-18a) and
then in the order of redemption (1:18b-20). Each part begins in
the original Greek with a "who is" clause (1:15a, 18b) that contains the word "firstborn"—"of all creation" (1:15a) and "from
the dead" (1:18b). Then there are reasons ("for") in 1:16 and
1:19, as well as conclusions in 1:17-18a and 1:20. The word "all"
runs through the whole text, serving as a basis for the later reflections on Christ's rule over all creation.

There is a consensus among biblical scholars that Colossians
1:15-20 contains an early Christian hymn about Christ as the
Wisdom of God and his role in creation and redemption. This
consensus is based on the unusual vocabulary, the parallel struc-
tures, the introductory relative clauses ("who is" in 1:15a and
1:18b), and the rhythmic quality of the language. However, the
hymn may have been slightly modified in the process of being
incorporated into the letter. The identification of the "body" in
1:18 as the church and the reference to "the blood of his cross" in
1:20 help to tie the hymn more directly into Christian life and the
Christ-event. The original hymn may have been used in the con-

text of a baptismal ceremony. This association is at least suggested by the introduction in 1:12-14 ("he has rescued us from the power of darkness"). In the context of the Letter to the Colossians, the hymn functions as the "text" to be explicated and developed in the rest of the letter.

The first part of the hymn (Colossians 1:15-18a) celebrates Christ as "the image of the invisible God" and "the firstborn of all creation." The biblical context of these descriptions is the personification of Wisdom as a female figure present at creation and now animating, permeating, and sustaining what God has created.

In Proverbs 8:22-31, Wisdom is described as being "at the beginning of his [God's] work" of creation and as observing and even taking part in that work "like a master worker." Her representation as a female figure reflects the gender of the Hebrew and Greek words for wisdom (*hokmah* and *sophia*). There may also be echoes of terms and concepts applied to goddesses in the ancient Near East, though in the Jewish context wisdom is an attribute of the God of Israel rather than a separate deity.

There is a similar presentation of Wisdom in Sirach 24, with the addition of the motif of Wisdom searching for a home or dwelling place on earth. She finds it at Mount Zion, in the Jerusalem Temple. The author goes on to equate Wisdom with "the book of the covenant of the Most High God, the law that Moses commanded us" (Sirach 24:23). In the Wisdom of Solomon, the figure of Wisdom is said to "fill the world" and "hold all things together" (Wisdom 1:7), functioning like a "world soul" animating all creation. She is also described as "a pure emanation of the glory of the Almighty . . . a reflection of eternal light, a spotless mirror of the working of God, and an image of his goodness" (7:25-26).

Despite their common themes, the biblical Wisdom texts do not present a uniform picture of what Wisdom is and where Wisdom is to be found. The first part of the hymn in Colossians 1:15-20 identifies Jesus Christ as the Wisdom of God and locates him both everywhere ("the body") and especially in the church. So the hymn represents the distinctively Christian contribution to the Jewish debate about the identity and the dwelling place of Wisdom.

The description of Christ as "the firstborn of all creation" in 1:15 evokes what is said of Wisdom in Proverbs 8:22: "The LORD created me at the beginning of his work." In Colossians the emphasis is on the superiority of Wisdom over creation rather than on the creaturehood of Wisdom. The point of the Christian hymn is to affirm that the one who is first in the order of creation is also the first in the order of redemption.

In the phrase "in him all things . . . were created" in Colossians 1:16, the introductory words "in him" are most likely instrumental, the equivalent of "through him" later in the verse. The claim echoes what is said in Proverbs 8:30 ("then I was beside him, like a master worker"). The list that follows in 1:16 emphasizes the sovereignty of Christ, the Wisdom of God, over all creation. Not only was Christ the instrument of their creation ("through him"), he was also the goal of their creation ("for him").

According to Colossians 1:17, Christ was not only at the origin of creation ("before all things") but he also keeps creation together in the present ("in him all things hold together"). Here the biblical context is the idea of Wisdom as a kind of "world soul" holding the world together and animating it, as in Wisdom 7:24: "Wisdom is more mobile than any motion; because of her pureness she pervades and penetrates all things."

Calling Christ in Colossians 1:18a "the head of the body" assumes that the world is a gigantic body directed by Wisdom. The "head" gives direction to the whole cosmos. The identification of the body as the church is a distinctively Christian interpretation of the image and gives the church a cosmic dimension beyond its existence in local communities.

The second part of the hymn (1:18b-20) reflects a more distinctively Christian theological context in that it takes as its starting point the resurrection of Jesus. Resurrection is, of course, a Jewish idea. Though there are many variations, the basic point is that at the end of human history as we know it and with the full coming of God's kingdom, God will raise up the dead and render a final judgment upon them—eternal life for the wise and righteous, and eternal punishment or annihilation for the wicked (see Daniel 12:1-3). That an individual should be resurrected to eternal life, as in the case of Jesus before the coming of God's kingdom in its fullness, went beyond Jewish beliefs about resurrection. The Christian claim is that in the resurrection of Jesus, God has anticipated or begun the process of bringing about the fullness of the kingdom.

The order of redemption (Colossians 1:18b-20) has been set in motion by the resurrection of Jesus Christ ("the firstborn from the dead"). His resurrection as the "first fruits" (see 1 Corinthians 15:20, 23) initiates the order of reconciliation and stands as the pledge for the general resurrection. The description of the risen Christ as having "first place in everything" means that just as in the order of creation Christ as the Wisdom of God was first, so in the order of redemption the risen Christ is first.

In later Gnostic writings, the "fullness" refers to the heavenly region between God and the world. But here in Colossians 1:19, the term does not carry that limited geographical sense. Here the idea is that the fullness of God (see 2:9) dwells in Christ. What God is, is present in Christ (see John 1:1, "the Word was God").

The verb "reconcile" in Colossians 1:20 refers to a change in relationships. Though generally used in the social or political spheres, here it appears in a cosmic context (see Romans 5:10-11; 11:15; 2 Corinthians 5:18-19). The effect of the expression "through the blood of his cross" is to specify Jesus' death on the cross as the means by which the cosmic reconciliation has taken place. The background is Leviticus 17:11 ("for, as life, it is the blood that makes atonement"). This theme is present in Romans 3:25 ("whom God put forward as a sacrifice of atonement by his blood") and in Hebrews 9:22 ("without the shedding of blood there is no forgiveness of sins").

JESUS CHRIST AS THE WORD OF GOD (JOHN 1:1-18)

In a drama, a "prologue" is an introductory speech, often in verse, that calls attention to the major themes in the play. John 1:1-18 fits that definition quite well. Much of the text follows the style of biblical poetry, with short units expressed in parallel lines and movement by association of words and ideas. In the context of John's Gospel as a whole, the prologue introduces many of the major ideas developed in the body of the gospel: Jesus' cosmic significance; his acceptance by some and rejection by others; his mission of revealing God as his heavenly Father; his ability to make people children of God, who can share in his special relationship with God; and his presence among us as the manifestation of God's glory.

The Johannine prologue very likely incorporates elements from an early Christian hymn now preserved in John 1:1-5, 10-14, and 16-18. The two parts of the prologue that concern John the Baptist (1:6-8, and 1:15) are written in prose rather than in poetry, and seem to have been added at some point to the poetic sections.

> ¹In the beginning was the Word, and the Word was with God, and the Word was God. ²He was in the beginning with

God. ³All things came into being through him, and without him not one thing came into being. What has come into being ⁴in him was life, and the life was the light of all people. ⁵The light shines in the darkness, and the darkness did not overcome it.

⁶There was a man sent from God, whose name was John. ⁷He came as a witness to testify to the light, so that all might believe through him. ⁸He himself was not the light, but he came to testify to the light. ⁹The true light, which enlightens everyone, was coming into the world.

¹⁰He was in the world, and the world came into being through him; yet the world did not know him. ¹¹He came to what was his own, and his own people did not accept him. ¹²But to all who received him, who believed in his name, he gave power to become children of God, ¹³who were born, not of blood or of the will of the flesh or of the will of man, but of God.

¹⁴And the Word became flesh and lived among us, and we have seen his glory, the glory as of a father's only son, full of grace and truth. ¹⁵(John testified to him and cried out, "This was he of whom I said, 'He who comes after me ranks ahead of me because he was before me.'") ¹⁶From his fullness we have all received, grace upon grace. ¹⁷The law indeed was given through Moses; grace and truth came through Jesus Christ. ¹⁸No one has ever seen God. It is God the only Son, who is close to the Father's heart, who has made him known.

(John 1:1-18)

The biblical context for the identification of Jesus Christ as the Word of God in John 1:1-18 seems to be the portrayal of

Wisdom as a personal figure, as was the case with the hymn in Colossians 1:15-20. According to Proverbs 8:22-26, Wisdom existed before the world was created ("In the beginning was the Word," John 1:1-5). Sirach 24:8-12 describes Wisdom dwelling among God's people, at the Jerusalem Temple ("the Word became flesh and lived among us," John 1:14). Wisdom 7:25-26 characterizes Wisdom as "a pure emanation of the glory of the Almighty . . . an image of his goodness" ("we have seen his glory," John 1:14) and as the one who reveals God ("It is God the only Son . . . who has made him known," John 1:18). What is said about Wisdom in the various biblical texts is said about Jesus, the Word of God, in the prologue to John's Gospel. The Word of God is the Wisdom of God. The wisdom that God wishes to reveal to us can be found in Jesus as the revealer and the revelation of God.

The first section of the Johannine prologue describes the Word of God before creation (1:1-2) and in creation (1:3-5). The opening phrase "in the beginning" deliberately recalls the opening words of Genesis, and the application of the title "Word" to Jesus recalls the creative power of God's word ("Then God said, 'Let there be light'; and there was light'") according to Genesis 1:3-5. There may be some connection to the concept of the Word (*Logos*) of God as a mediator between God and creation that was developed especially by Philo of Alexandria, a first-century Jewish writer who sought to join concepts from the Old Testament and Greek philosophy. But the most important piece of biblical context remains the portrayal of Wisdom as a personal figure. As the Wisdom of God, Jesus was with God in the beginning. However, the prologue goes beyond its biblical models first by calling Jesus the "Word," and then by affirming his divinity ("and the Word was God"). As God's Word, he communicates what was on God's mind to reveal. Throughout the Fourth Gospel, Jesus reveals his heavenly Father by word and action. And the gospel reaches its climax when Thomas identifies Jesus as "my Lord and my God" (20:28).

As God's agent in creation (John 1:3-5), the Word was responsible for "life" and "light"—fitting terms for the one who will emerge as the life (11:25) and the light (8:12) during his public ministry. The contrast between light and darkness (1:5) not only recalls the creation story (Genesis 1:3-5), but also sets the stage for Jesus' struggle on behalf of the children of light against the powers of darkness. So from the first part of the prologue we learn about Jesus' identity, his cosmic significance, and the conflict that will shape his life. The first prose section about John the Baptist (1:6-8) emphasizes his subordinate role as a witness to Jesus.

The description of Jesus as the Light coming into the world in John 1:9-11 gives particular attention to the negative reception that Jesus received from the world and from his own people. As the man from heaven, Jesus was sent to reveal God. But neither "the world" nor "his own people" accepted him (1:10-11). Throughout the Fourth Gospel, the opponents of Jesus are frequently referred to as "the world" and "the Jews." Of course, all the earliest followers of Jesus were Jews themselves, and so "his own people" may mean many of his own people but surely not all without exception. The point is that opposition to Jesus is expressed even in the prologue.

The coming of God's Son into the world has made it possible for others to become children of God through faith (John 1:12-13). This new status must be viewed as God's gift rather than as a right or an acquisition. Some ancient manuscripts read the verb as a singular ("who was born") and make the sentence into a reference to Jesus' own virginal conception ("who was born . . . of

God"). But the plural reading is much better attested. Through him we too can become God's children.

The second description of the Word's coming into the world in John 1:14 uses two powerful images: incarnation ("the Word became flesh") and tabernacling ("lived among us"; literally, "pitched his tent"). Without ceasing to be the Word of God or becoming anything less, the Word became flesh (see 1 John 4:2; 2 John 7). The tabernacle or tent of meeting according to Exodus 25:8-9 was the place of God's presence among the people of Israel. Whereas the first description of the Word's coming in John 1:9-11 as Light into the world stressed his negative reception, the second description focuses on the positive reception of him ("we have seen his glory"). The terms "grace and truth" reflect the covenant relationship between God and his people (see Exodus 34:6). As God's only Son, Jesus is the full manifestation of God's glory that previously had only been glimpsed in Israel's history. The second prose parenthesis about John the Baptist in 1:15 again acknowledges Jesus' superiority on the grounds of his pre-existence ("he was before me").

The role of Jesus as the Word of God in the history of salvation is taken up again in John 1:16-18. The covenant with Moses was a "grace," an act of divine favor, and the Law revealed through Moses to Israel was also a gift. Without rejecting those gifts, the prologue insists that Jesus was a "grace upon grace" (1:16). It also maintains that he has brought about the "grace and truth" between God and his people that was the goal of the covenant relationship between God and ancient Israel. In the body of the Fourth Gospel, Jesus neither annuls nor replaces the Scriptures of Israel. Rather, they reach their fulfillment in him (see 5:39). The major function of Jesus as the Word of God was to reveal God: "It is God the only Son, who is close to the Father's heart, who has made him known" (1:18). Although John perceived the Father and the Son as distinct, he ascribed divinity to both of them (see 1:1; 20:28). The task of the Son in his time on earth was to reveal God to human beings and so to open up the way toward the Father. How he fulfilled that task is the main topic in the body of John's Gospel. The Son is now back again (literally, "in the bosom of") with the Father.

EARLY CHRISTIAN CONFESSIONS OF FAITH

The early Christian hymns about Jesus that are preserved in the New Testament provide us with precious glimpses into what early Christians believed about Jesus. They identify and praise Jesus as the Servant of the Lord, the Wisdom of God, and the Word of God. Sprinkled through the Pauline letters are other precious resources for our better understanding of what early Christians believed about Jesus. They are brief credal statements or capsule summaries of Christian faith. They are not technically prayers of praise or of petition. But their form and content mark them as statements that were easy to memorize and so could serve as the equivalent of short prayers reminding early Christians about who Jesus was and why he was so important. In this respect, they are something like the Jewish recitation of the *Shema* or like the Christian professions of faith (such as the Apostles' Creed).

These miniature summaries of early Christian faith are sprinkled throughout Paul's letters. Paul's undisputed letters are the earliest complete documents contained in the New Testament, having been composed in the 50s of the first century A.D., some twenty-five years after Jesus' death. They reflect the amazingly quick development of the Christian theological vocabulary and conceptuality. So rapid was this development that it is better described as an explosion than as a development. Paul included these credal statements at pivotal points in his letters. His strategic use of them assumes that his first readers were also aware of them and accepted them, and that they could provide common ground between Paul and his readers.

In dealing with problems associated with the resurrection of Jesus and its significance for Christians at Corinth, Paul points at the outset of his argument in 1 Corinthians 15 to what he himself had received as a summary of Christian faith and what he had then handed on to the Corinthian Christians when he brought Christianity to them: "that Christ died for our sins in accordance with the scriptures, and that he was buried, and that he was raised on the third day in accordance with the scriptures, and that he appeared to Cephas, then to the twelve" (15:3-5). The statement focuses on the saving significance of Jesus' death and resurrection and insists that these events took place in accord with the Old Testament Scriptures. And it declares that the risen Jesus appeared to his followers, who can verify that they experienced him as alive again.

In writing to the Galatians, Paul was trying to convince them that the claim being made by rival Jewish Christian missionaries that Gentiles had to become Jews in order to be real Christians was incorrect. One of his strategies was to show with appeals to several biblical texts in Galatians 3 that the real children of Abraham—and thus the real Christians—were those who imitated Abraham's example of faith. To clinch his argument, Paul near the end quotes what seems to have been an early Christian baptismal slogan: "There is no longer Jew or Greek, there is no longer slave or free, there is no longer male and female; for all of you are one in Christ Jesus" (3:28). Without necessarily abolishing these very real social differences, the statement asserts that being "in Christ" through faith and baptism renders these distinctions of at best secondary importance. And it insists that before God, what counts is participation in the mystery of Jesus' death and resurrection. The fact that in his argument in Galatians 3, Paul was mainly interested in the phrase "no longer Jew or Greek" indicates that he was calling upon a formulation that was already fixed and well known to other early Christians.

The longest and most famous of Paul's letters is his Epistle to the Romans. His other letters were sent to communities that he himself had founded, and so were extensions of his pastoral care for them. But when Paul wrote to the Romans, he had never been to Rome, nor had he a role in founding the Christian community there. Rather, Paul hoped to visit with the Romans briefly before moving on to a new mission in Spain. His letter was his way of introducing himself and his gospel to the community at Rome, asking for their hospitality, and offering some advice on problems that were dividing Jewish and Gentile Christians there.

In his salutation to the Romans, Paul in 1:3-4 defines the gospel in this way: "the gospel concerning his Son, who was descended from David according to the flesh and was declared to be Son of God with power according to the spirit of holiness by resurrection from the dead, Jesus Christ our Lord." The parallelism and the use of the odd expression "the spirit of holiness" for the Holy Spirit suggest that Paul was quoting a fixed formula well known both to him and to the Roman Christians. The statement captures the humanity of Jesus and his Jewish roots ("descended from David according to the flesh"), while pointing to the resurrection as the pivotal event in which Jesus' true identity as the Son of God and the Lord was made manifest.

In Romans 3:25, when Paul was winding up his argument that all people—Gentiles and Jews alike—needed the revelation of

God's righteousness in Christ, he describes the saving significance of Jesus' death in the following way: "whom God put forward as a sacrifice of atonement by his blood, effective through faith. He did this to show his righteousness, because in his divine forbearance he had passed over the sins previously committed." Again the unusual vocabulary marks this as an already existing formula. It interprets the death of Jesus as a sacrifice expiating or atoning for the sins of humankind, and as the means by which right relationship with God (justification) has been made possible for all people of faith. The clause "effective through faith" may be Paul's own addition to the formula, since it expresses the very point he wants to emphasize in this part of his letter.

The pastoral epistles (1 and 2 Timothy and Titus) were written either by Paul himself late in his career in the 60s of the first century or more likely by an admirer in the late first century. They offer advice to pastors—Timothy and Titus—about church offices and other practical aspects of Christian life, and so for several centuries they have been called the "pastorals." Rather than engaging in extended theological reflections as Paul often does, they tend to call on preexisting credal statements to motivate Christians and to end controversies. These statements are often preceded or followed by a formula that indicates their importance and authority. For example in 1 Timothy 1:15 we read, "The saying is sure and worthy of full acceptance, that Christ Jesus came into the world to save sinners."

A more extensive credal statement appears in 1 Timothy 2:5-6: "For there is one God; / there is also one mediator between God and humankind, / Christ Jesus, himself human, / who gave himself a ransom for all." The statement emphasizes the humanity of Jesus, his role as mediator between God and humankind, and the saving and expiatory value of his death on the cross. The image of the "ransom" continues the theme of the sacrificial dimension of Jesus' death in making possible right relationship with God.

A relatively more elaborate summary of Christian faith appears in 1 Timothy 3:16. It is introduced as a statement of "the mystery of our religion":

> [16]Without any doubt, the mystery of our religion is great:
>   He was revealed in flesh,
>   vindicated in spirit,
>   seen by angels,
>   proclaimed among Gentiles,
>   believed in throughout the world,
>   taken up in glory.
> (1 Timothy 3:16)

It consists of six members, arranged in an ABCCBA pattern. It refers to the incarnation and exaltation of Jesus (AA), the resurrection as vindication of him and the faith that he has inspired throughout the world (BB), and his having been seen by angels and proclaimed among non-Jews (CC).

Another "sure" saying appears in 2 Timothy 2:11–13:

> [11]The saying is sure:
>   If we have died with him, we will also live with him;
>   [12]if we endure, we will also reign with him;
>   if we deny him, he will also deny us;
>   [13]if we are faithless, he remains faithful—
>   for he cannot deny himself.
> (2 Timothy 2:11-13)

Its four phrases trace the possible path of Christian life from baptism, through suffering and denial under persecution, to faithlessness. But it insists that no matter how unfaithful we may prove to be, Christ Jesus will remain faithful to us.

While not strictly prayers in their literary form, these summaries of faith in Paul's letters and in the pastorals very likely functioned as prayers for early Christians, as they can for us. They are short, rhythmic, and memorable. They cover various aspects of Christ's life (his incarnation, suffering, death, resurrection, and exaltation); the saving significance of his death and resurrection (sacrifice for sins, ransom); and the responses that the risen Christ should elicit from believers (faith, gratitude, fidelity, and hope).

Bringing the Contexts Together

The hymns and credal statements treated in this chapter provide eloquent testimony to the explosion of beliefs about Jesus in the twenty or so years after his death. Given the shameful nature of crucifixion as a gruesome punishment visited upon rebels and slaves, it is all the more remarkable that early Christians very quickly came to celebrate Jesus as Lord (Philippians 2:6-11), the Wisdom of God (Colossians 1:15-20), and the Word of God (John 1:1-18), and that they regarded his death on the cross as the perfect sacrifice for sins and as the event that has made right relationship with God (justification) possible. Two thousand years later we can only marvel at those developments and attribute them to the power of Jesus' resurrection.

It is said that those who sing pray twice. The texts treated here and Pliny's testimony about early Christian worship services indicate that communal singing was part of Christian prayer from earliest times. The hymnic prayer texts and credal formulas preserved in the New Testament put us in touch with the faith experiences and convictions of the earliest Christians. They indicate the difference that Christ made in their lives and the new context in which they placed their lives. They challenge us today to compose and sing hymns and to profess our faith in ways that both stand firmly in the great tradition of biblical faith and speak to people of good will in the twenty-first century.

Think, Pray, and Act

Consider how the hymns and credal statements in the New Testament might enrich your appreciation of Jesus and your own way of praying.

Think
§ Why do most Christian liturgies include music?

§ What does it mean for you to call Jesus Lord, Wisdom, and the Word of God?

§ Why are the short credal statements scattered throughout the Pauline letters so important?

Pray
§ Read the three early Christian hymns treated above slowly and meditatively, and ask God to help you to appreciate more fully the significance of Jesus Christ.

§ Meditate on the various credal formulas treated above and ask God to help you to appreciate more fully what God has done in Christ.

Act

§ At the next liturgical event in which you participate, try to take even more consciously and seriously the opportunity to sing the praises of God and Christ and to profess your faith.

Chapter Five

Pauline Prayers

Paul was the first great theologian of the early Christian movement, and his letters (written in the 50s of the first century A.D.) are the earliest complete documents in the New Testament. However, Paul was not a professor or a philosopher. Rather, he defined his vocation as bringing the good news about Jesus Christ to peoples and places where the gospel had not yet been heard (see Romans 15:14-21). Most of his letters were ways of overseeing the continuing growth and development of the communities he had founded, and can greatly enrich our understanding and practice of Christian prayer.

So Paul was primarily a founder of Christian communities. When he perceived that a church that he had founded was sufficiently well established, he moved on to other cities. Of the twenty-seven writings that comprise the New Testament, thirteen are letters attributed to Paul. And more than half of the Acts of the Apostles is devoted to Paul's missionary activities. In his letters, Paul dealt primarily with the pastoral problems that had arisen in his absence. So Paul is best described as a pastoral theologian. That is, Paul worked out his theology in the context of the problems that concerned the Christians in the communities that he had founded.

Biblical scholars today often distinguish between the seven "undisputed" and the six "disputed" Pauline letters in the New Testament. Hardly any scholar today disputes that Paul, with some help from co-workers and scribes, wrote the seven letters known as Romans, 1 and 2 Corinthians, Galatians, Philippians, 1 Thessalonians, and Philemon. Many scholars, however, contend that 2 Thessalonians, Ephesians, Colossians, 1 and 2 Timothy, and Titus may have been written in Paul's name later in the first century as a way of carrying on Paul's apostolic ministry. Of course, all thirteen letters belong to the Christian canon of the New Testament and are recognized as Sacred Scripture by all the churches.

Pauline Thanksgivings

The thanksgivings near the beginning of most Pauline letters were part of the epistolary convention found in many letters from the Greco-Roman world. A typical letter first identified the sender and the recipient, and then offered a greeting. Next the writer would usually insert a prayer or a thanksgiving for the good health and/or good fortune of the recipient.

While observing these letter-writing conventions, Paul also adapted them for his own theological and pastoral purposes. In his salutations and greetings, Paul does not hesitate to expand the various elements—sender, addressee, and greeting. He develops them to establish his apostolic authority, to help the recipients to recognize their dignity in Christ, and to anticipate themes to be developed in the body of the letter. Likewise, in his thanksgivings Paul generally thanks God for the gift of faith that these people have received and prays that they will grow in faith, love, and hope. He makes frequent use of the verbs "thank," "remember," and "pray." And he often takes the occasion to introduce themes that he wishes to emphasize in the body of the letter. In this way the Pauline thanksgivings, while part of the customs involved in writing letters in Greco-Roman antiquity, become genuine prayers offered by the apostle on behalf of those whom he had brought to Christian faith. The Pauline thanksgivings remind us all that as Christians, we can and should remember, pray for, and thank God for one another.

The shortest of the undisputed Pauline letters is the Epistle to Philemon. It contains only twenty-five verses. Paul wrote this letter from prison, perhaps at Ephesus. He identifies his co-worker Timothy as his coauthor, though he quickly switches into first-person singular language ("I"). The letter is addressed primarily to someone named Philemon, but is also directed to Apphia ("our sister"), Archippus ("our fellow soldier"), and "the church in your house." Philemon seems to have been a wealthy man, wealthy enough to own a large house, probably at Colossae, that might serve as a gathering place for thirty or forty fellow Christians. Apphia was most likely his wife, and Archippus seems to have been a Christian well known to both Paul and Philemon. While addressed to these three persons, the letter was also intended to be read aloud before the whole community gathered together in Philemon's house.

The situation that occasioned Paul's letter to Philemon was sensitive and complicated. The economy of the Roman Empire was based to a large extent on slavery. Large percentages of the population were slaves, and the problem of runaway slaves was taken very seriously. It appears that Onesimus, a slave belonging to Philemon, had run away, perhaps after being caught in some financial mismanagement. Onesimus eventually found his way to Paul in prison and under Paul's guidance had become a Christian. The purpose of his letter was to ask Philemon to take Onesimus back into his household "no longer as a slave but more than a slave, a beloved brother" (verse 16).

Whether Paul expected Philemon to free Onesimus is not clear. If he did, Philemon would run the risk of having other slaves run away and do the same thing. At the very least, however, Paul expected that Philemon would no longer look upon Onesimus simply as a piece of property, but rather as an equal in the sight of God (see Galatians 3:28). In making his case Paul reminds Philemon of the spiritual debt owed to the apostle for bringing him to Christian faith.

Before getting into the body of the letter and giving the reasons why Paul hoped that Philemon might comply with his request, Paul offers in verses 4-7 his prayer in which he thanks God especially for Philemon's love and faith.

> 4When I remember you in my prayers, I always thank my God 5because I hear of your love for all the saints and your faith toward the Lord Jesus. 6I pray that the sharing of your faith may become effective when you perceive all the good that we may do for Christ. 7I have indeed received much joy and encouragement from your love, because the hearts of the saints have been refreshed through you, my brother. (Philemon 1:4-7)

Paul's thanksgiving here and elsewhere in his letters is not exactly a formal prayer like the Old Testament and early Jewish thanksgiving hymns (see also Matthew 11:25-26), since it is not directly addressed to God. Rather, Paul describes to Philemon and his fellow church members what were his prayers of thanksgiving and petition on their behalf. The description of how he has given thanks to God in his own prayer serves a double purpose. On the one hand, it acknowledges and even flatters Philemon for past expressions of his love and faith. On the other hand, it puts pressure on Philemon to do what Paul is asking of him. Even though as an apostle Paul had great moral authority, he refuses to command Philemon. Instead, he wants to persuade Philemon that taking Onesimus back as "a beloved brother" would be an appropriate way of expressing his well-known gifts of love and faith.

There is, however, no need to doubt Paul's sincerity or to dismiss his thanksgiving as a mere rhetorical ploy. On the contrary, there is every reason to assume that Paul prayed fervently that the outcome of his letter would be positive for both Onesimus and Philemon. We can safely believe that Paul expected his prayer to inspire his friend Philemon to prove once more his love and faith toward the Lord Jesus by coming to regard his runaway slave as "a beloved brother" in Christ. The name "Onesimus" means "useful." But through his mismanagement and flight Onesimus had become useless to Philemon. Through his conversion, however, Onesimus had become useful to Paul. And it was Paul's hope that Onesimus might once again become useful—and even more—to Philemon.

OTHER PAULINE THANKSGIVINGS

Paul's First Letter to the Thessalonians is generally regarded as having been composed in A.D. 50 or 51, and thus as the earliest complete document in the New Testament. The thanksgiving found in 1 Thessalonians 1:2-3 set the pattern for the thanksgivings found in the other Pauline letters.

> [2]We always give thanks to God for all of you and mention you in our prayers, constantly [3]remembering before our God and Father your work of faith and labor of love and steadfastness of hope in our Lord Jesus Christ.
> (1 Thessalonians 1:2-3)

The verbs "thank," "pray," and "remember" are prominent. Jesus is referred to with the very reverential title "our Lord Jesus Christ." And the three virtues singled out for special mention provide the outline to be developed in the body of the letter: faith (1:4–3:10), love (3:11–4:12), and hope (4:13–5:11). This triad of theological virtues has become a fixed point in the Christian theological tradition, and it appears here first in Paul's account of his thanksgiving for what the Thessalonian Christians had achieved by way of progress in the Christian life.

In the Letter to the Galatians, there is no thanksgiving. That was Paul's not-so-subtle way of expressing at the outset his displeasure that the Gentile Christians in Galatia were allowing other Jewish Christian missionaries to persuade them that Paul's gospel was wrong, and that they had to become Jews in order to be real Christians. Rather, Paul expresses his astonishment at them for turning to "a different gospel" (1:6), and later calls them "foolish" and even "bewitched" (3:1).

In 1 Corinthians 1:4-9, Paul gives thanks for "the grace of God that has been given you in Christ Jesus." He also prays that the Corinthian Christians not "be lacking in any spiritual gift as you wait for the revealing of our Lord Jesus Christ" (1:7). One of the topics running through 1 Corinthians is the division within the community over the origin and use of the spiritual gifts or charisms. So in his opening thanksgiving, Paul emphasizes that God is the origin of all spiritual gifts and that the fullness of life in the Spirit will take place with the fullness of God's kingdom. In 2 Corinthians Paul opens the letter with a benediction or blessing (see the next section) rather than a thanksgiving.

Paul wrote to the Philippians because they were experiencing tensions in their community. One of the purposes of Paul's letter was to get them to show greater respect to one another. In particular there seems to have been some quarrel between two women named Euodia and Syntyche, and thus Paul pleaded that they might be "of the same mind in the Lord." So in the thanksgiving that opens his letter to the Philippians, Paul, after using the words "thank," "remember," and "pray," expresses his special thanks for "your sharing in the gospel from the first day until now" (1:5). Thus he hints that the gospel centered on Jesus' death and resurrection (see 2:6-11) is and should be the basis of fellowship (*koinonia*) within the Christian community.

Paul had not founded the Christian community in Rome, nor had he ever visited that city when he wrote to the Roman Christians in A.D. 57 or 58. Rather, Christianity originated in Rome very early within the large Jewish community there. In writing to the Romans, Paul was introducing himself and his gospel, though the Roman Christians surely had heard about him. After an extended and elaborate salutation (Romans 1:1-7), Paul begins his thanksgiving by noting that "your faith is proclaimed throughout the world" (1:8). As the capital of the Roman Empire, the city of Rome was well known throughout the ancient world. And likewise the Roman Christian community would have been a topic of interest to the other Christians spread throughout the empire. Thus Paul would have been acknowledging the importance of the church at Rome and rendering the recipients open toward him and his rather bold initiative in writing them such a long and wide-ranging letter. Moreover, one of Paul's purposes in writing to the Romans seems to have been to defuse tensions between Jewish Christians and Gentile Christians there. Reminding both groups that the whole church and the whole empire were watching them was a good rhetorical strategy to get their attention and make them work at resolving their differences.

The thanksgiving is also part of most of the "Deuteropauline" letters, that is, New Testament letters that probably were written by later followers of Paul. In 2 Thessalonians 1:3, the writer thanks God because "your faith is growing abundantly and the love of everyone of you for one another is increasing." The elements of hope prominent in Paul's thanksgiving in 1 Thessalonians are developed immediately in the instruction about the last judgment and the second coming of Christ in 1:5-10.

The Letter to the Colossians emphasizes the absolute sufficiency of Jesus' death and resurrection to bring about right relationship with God and the definitive revelation of God's wisdom in Jesus as the Wisdom of God (see 1:15-20). The thanksgiving in 1:3-14 mentions the faith, love, and hope of the Colossians: "for we have heard of your faith in Christ Jesus and of the love that you have for all the saints, because of the hope laid up for you in heaven" (1:4-5). It also introduces the main theme to be developed in the first half of the letter: "that you may be filled with the knowledge of God's will in all spiritual wisdom and understanding" (1:9).

In the Letter to the Ephesians, the thanksgiving (1:15-23) follows a long benediction in 1:3-14 (see the next section on Pauline benedictions). After noting what he had heard about their faith and love ("your faith in the Lord Jesus and your love toward all the saints," 1:15), the author prays that they may come to enjoy the fullness of "the hope to which he [God] has called you" (1:18). How they may come to experience the fullness of that hope is described in the body of the letter, which explores the cosmic significance of Jesus' death and resurrection and the worldwide scope of the body of Christ, which is the church.

While the pastoral letters known as 1 Timothy and Titus do not contain formal thanksgivings, what is presented as Paul's farewell letter or testament in 2 Timothy contains in 1:3-7 the usual terms ("thank," "pray," and "remember") and introduces the theme of rekindling the gift of God (charism) that came to Timothy with his "ordination" at Paul's hands. The body of 2 Timothy encourages Timothy to respond to the pastoral challenges he will face as Paul's apostolic delegate in Ephesus.

PAULINE BENEDICTIONS

As we saw with Zechariah's *Benedictus* in Luke 1:68-79, a benediction is a prayer of praise with regard to God ("Blessed be the Lord God of Israel") along with a reason why God is worthy of such praise ("for he has looked favorably on his people and redeemed them"). The blessing formula ("Blessed be . . ."; *baruk* in Hebrew) appears in Psalm 119:12 ("Blessed are you, O LORD") and in Tobit 13:1 ("Blessed be God who lives forever, because his kingdom lasts throughout all ages"). It also occurs in many other biblical (see, for example, Psalm 41:13; 72:18-19; 1 Kings 8:15, 56) and early Jewish texts, including the Dead Sea scrolls (see *Community Rule* 11:15). In rabbinic Judaism from the second century onward, the *berakah* or "benediction" became the most common Jewish prayer form. It was used not only in the formal communal prayers like the Eighteen Benedictions ("Blessed are you, O Lord . . .") but also in grace before meals ("Blessed are you, O Lord our God, King of the universe, who brings forth food from the earth . . .") and at many other occasions in everyday life.

Paul's Second Letter to the Corinthians contains a benediction (1:3-7) instead of a thanksgiving. The introductory formula has been adapted to express what early Christians had come to believe about Jesus and his Father: "Blessed be the God and Father of our Lord Jesus Christ, the Father of mercies and the God of all consolation" (1:3). The Greek root for "console" (*parakaleo*) appears ten times as either a verb or a noun in this benediction. The idea is that since the God of all consolation has consoled Paul and Timothy in their sufferings, so they are able to console others in their sufferings. Just as Christ's sufferings are abundant, so the apostles' consolation in Christ is abundant.

The benediction provides the occasion for Paul in 2 Corinthians 1:8-11 to launch into a description of "the affliction we experienced in Asia." Here "Asia" refers to the province of Asia Minor. Large parts of 2 Corinthians concern the defense of Paul's apostleship and the gospel that he preached in response to attacks against him from other Jewish Christians. Throughout the body of the letter Paul appeals often to his personal sufferings for the sake of the gospel, culminating in his catalogue of sufferings in 11:23-29 and his references to his mysterious "thorn in the flesh" (12:7). So at the very beginning of 2 Corinthians, Paul uses the benediction formula to introduce the themes of affliction (or suffering) and consolation that are very prominent in the body of the letter.

The opening chapter in the Letter to the Ephesians contains both a benediction (1:3-14) and a thanksgiving (1:15-23). The benediction is one long sentence, the longest sentence in the New Testament. Its rich and repetitive language makes it sound like a hymn. But it is more likely a prose composition intended to have the effect of a hymn. As a benediction it is a prayer of praise regarding what God has done for us in and through Christ. As a response to the benefits that God has bestowed on us through Jesus' life, death, and resurrection (the paschal mystery), this benediction praises God as the benefactor *par excellence*.

While probably not composed directly by Paul, the benediction in Ephesians 1:3-14 is an apt summary of Paul's theology, since Paul was primarily interested in what God has done for us in Christ. This topic is what theologians call "soteriology," that is, the saving significance of Jesus for us. There is an old theory that Ephesians was originally composed by an admirer of Paul as an introduction to a collection of Paul's letters. At the very least, that theory underlines the close relationship between Paul's own theology and that in Ephesians. In this benediction, the focus shifts in turn from God the Father (1:3-6) to the Son (1:7-12) and then to the Holy Spirit (1:13-14), though of course there is no rigid separation among the persons of the Trinity and their actions.

> [3]Blessed be the God and Father of our Lord Jesus Christ, who has blessed us in Christ with every spiritual blessing in the heavenly places, [4]just as he chose us in Christ before the foundation of the world to be holy and blameless before him in love. [5]He destined us for adoption as his children through Jesus Christ, according to the good pleasure of his will, [6]to the praise of his glorious grace that he freely bestowed on us in the Beloved. [7]In him we have redemption through his blood, the forgiveness of our trespasses, according to the riches of his grace [8]that he lavished on us. With all wisdom and insight [9] he has made known to us the mystery of his will, according to his good pleasure that he set forth in Christ, [10]as a plan for the fullness of time, to gather up all things in him, things in heaven and things on earth. [11]In Christ we have also obtained an inheritance, having been destined according to the purpose of him who accomplishes all things according to his counsel and will, [12]so that we, who were the first to set our hope on Christ, might live for the praise of his glory. [13]In him you also, when you had heard the word of truth, the gospel of your

salvation, and had believed in him, were marked with the seal of the promised Holy Spirit; [14]this is the pledge of our inheritance toward redemption as God's own people, to the praise of his glory.
(Ephesians 1:3-14)

This prayer of praise to God as our great benefactor first notes God's gifts of election and adoption (Ephesians 1:3-6), that is, the special favors or graces that God has shown to those who are in Christ. These statements bring up the theological problem of predestination (see also Romans 8:29-30). But the point here is a positive one: God has manifested a special care for those who are in Christ by choosing them and making them his children even before they existed. Throughout the benediction, there is a stress on God's grace and favor toward us.

The benediction goes on in Ephesians 1:7-12 to praise God for the gifts of redemption and forgiveness of sins "through his [Christ's] blood," as well as wisdom or insight into the divine plan of salvation ("the mystery of his will"), according to which all things have been gathered up or "recapitulated" in Christ (see Colossians 1:19-20). Moreover, through Christ, we have the hope of obtaining our "inheritance," that is, eternal life with God.

In 1:13-14 the language switches to the first-person plural ("we") and the focus shifts to the ongoing work of the Holy Spirit. It traces the process through which the readers of the letter have passed: hearing the word of truth (the gospel that brings salvation); believing in Christ and his Father (coming to faith); and being marked with "the seal of the promised Holy Spirit" (in baptism). The reception of the Holy Spirit is described in Greek as the *arrabon* ("pledge, first installment, down payment") of the

fullness of eternal life with God ("our inheritance"). The benediction ends as it began, with a word of praise for God ("to the
praise of his [God's] glory").

THE HOLY SPIRIT'S ROLE IN PRAYER

In writing to the Romans in the 50s of the first century A.D., Paul
sought to help the Jewish Christians and Gentile Christians there
to respect one another as equals before God. The main topic of the
letter to the Romans is "the gospel," which for Paul meant the saving or soteriological significance of Jesus' death and resurrection.
In the midpoint of his letter (chapter 8), Paul reflects on the gospel
and life "in the spirit." There is always some ambiguity in Paul's
use of the term "spirit" (*pneuma* in Greek). The earliest Greek
manuscripts were written entirely in capital letters, and so transla-
tors have to look to the context to decide which usage is meant. In
some cases, *pneuma* refers to the Holy Spirit, while in other cases
it refers to that aspect of the human person —the spiritual dimension—that is open to the promptings of the Holy Spirit.

The context of Paul's teaching on the Holy Spirit's role in our
prayer is Paul's meditation on life in the spirit/Spirit in Romans 8.
Thus far in his letter, Paul has shown that all humans—Jews and
Gentiles alike—needed the revelation of God's righteousness or
justice in Christ (chapters 1–3). He has demonstrated that faith
after the pattern set by Abraham is the way by which we all can
enter into that revelation (chapter 4). And he has established that
through Jesus' death and resurrection, we have been delivered
from domination by sin, death, and the law (chapters 5–7) and
freed for life in the spirit/Spirit (chapter 8).

After describing how the Holy Spirit empowers us to live in the
"spirit" (Romans 8:1-11), Paul explains how Christians can be

called children of God (8:12-17) and reflects on the present and future dimensions and the individual and cosmic dimensions of Christian life (8:18-25). Then he presents his teaching about the Holy Spirit's role in our prayer (8:26-27) and affirms that God is for us and with us (8:28-39). In this context, Paul in 8:26-27 identifies the Holy Spirit as the primary agent in Christian prayer:

> [26]Likewise the Spirit helps us in our weakness; for we do not know how to pray as we ought, but that very Spirit intercedes with sighs too deep for words. [27]And God, who searches the heart, knows what is the mind of the Spirit, because the Spirit intercedes for the saints according to the will of God.
> (Romans 8:26-27)

There are three main characters in this short passage: the Holy Spirit, those who pray, and God the Father. The Holy Spirit helps those who pray and makes sure that God hears their prayers. The Spirit of God works with and especially through our human "weakness," which is a way of expressing the unfinished or "not yet" dimension of Christ's redemptive work. The Spirit also works through the lingering effects of the power of sin and death upon and within us. The "sighs too deep for words" or "inexpressible groanings" that accompany prayer are both a sign of human weakness and a proof that the intercession of the Holy Spirit is needed when we pray. Some interpreters find in this expression a critical comment aimed at those early Christians who wrongly in Paul's view regarded speaking in "tongues" as the height of spiritual accomplishment (see 1 Corinthians 12-14).

In Romans 8:27 "the one who searches the heart" is most likely God the Father (see 1 Samuel 16:7; 1 Kings 8:39; 1 Chronicles

28:9; Psalms 7:10; 17:3; 139:1), who works in cooperation with the Holy Spirit. Another interpretation takes the Holy Spirit as the one who searches the heart and so has the "Spirit" working in cooperation with the human "spirit." The "saints" or "holy ones" is a title commonly applied not only to early Christians but also to members of the Dead Sea sect. It refers first of all to God as the Holy One who communicates his holiness to humans, thus enabling them to be called "saints."

Romans 8:26-27 makes an important contribution to our understanding of the Trinity and develops rich theological themes, such as our human weakness before God, God as the one who searches the heart, and Christians as "saints." But most important of all is its insistence on what God and the Holy Spirit do when we pray.

PAULINE DOXOLOGIES

A doxology is "a word of praise." It usually contains four elements: a mention of the person or deity to be praised, usually in the Greek dative case ("to . . ."); a word of praise, usually including the word "glory" (*doxa* in Greek); an indication of time or eternity ("forever"); and a closing response of acceptance or affirmation ("Amen") in which the hearers make the prayer of praise their own. In the New Testament, doxologies generally serve to conclude a document or a unit within a document. Today we often use the doxology "Glory to the Father and to the Son . . ." in a similar way.

The literary form of the doxology is presented at its simplest level in the Greek Bible's Prayer of Manasseh 15: "and yours [God's] is the glory forever. Amen." Likewise in 4 Maccabees 18:24, also in the Greek Bible, there is a very short example of a doxology: "to whom [God] be glory forever and ever. Amen." Perhaps the most familiar doxology appears at the end of the Lord's Prayer in Matthew 6:13 in some later and inferior manuscripts: "For yours [God's] are the kingdom and the power and the glory forever. Amen."

The doxology that concludes the text of the Letter to the Romans in 16:25-27 is generally regarded as an addition to Paul's letter. In style and vocabulary it is quite different from what appears in the body of the letter. However, its praise of God for revealing the mystery of salvation in Christ does correspond nicely with the gospel, which is the basic content of Romans.

> [25]Now to God who is able to strengthen you according to my gospel and the proclamation of Jesus Christ, according to the revelation of the mystery that was kept secret for long ages [26]but is now disclosed, and through the prophetic writings is made known to all the Gentiles, according to the command of the eternal God, to bring about the obedience of faith— [27]to the only wise God, through Jesus Christ, to whom be the glory forever! Amen.
> (Romans 16:25-27)

In the Letter to the Ephesians, the doxology in 3:20-21 serves as a conclusion to the first part of the letter by giving praise and thanks to God for the success of the Pauline mission. In particular, it concludes the text of what is presented as Paul's own prayer in 3:14-19 that God may strengthen the readers through the Holy Spirit, that Christ may dwell in their hearts, and that they may understand the universal scope of the love of Christ and be filled with all the fullness of God.

[20]Now to him who by the power at work within us is able to accomplish abundantly far more than all we can ask or imagine, [21]to him be glory in the church and in Christ Jesus to all generations, forever and ever. Amen.
(Ephesians 3:20-21)

In 1 Timothy 1:17 Paul's words of thanks for God's mercy in forgiving his sins end with a doxology: "To the King of the ages, immortal, invisible, the only God, be honor and glory forever and ever. Amen." And just before the final greetings there is another short doxology that closes off Paul's words of thanks to God for standing by him in his trials and rescuing him, "To him be the glory forever and ever. Amen" (2 Timothy 4:18). Still another good example of a doxology in the New Testament appears in the Letter of Jude:

[24] Now to him who is able to keep you from falling, and to make you stand without blemish in the presence of his glory with rejoicing, [25] to the only God our Savior, through Jesus Christ our Lord, be glory, majesty, power, and authority, before all time and now and forever. Amen.
(Jude 1:24-25)

Here the emphasis is on God's ability to sustain Christians in preparation for the last judgment. It fits well with the many references to the last judgment throughout the Letter of Jude.

Bringing the Contexts Together

Paul in his letters makes substantial additions to the categories of Christian prayer: thanksgivings, benedictions, and doxologies.

While they all are expressions of praise to God, they express their praise in slightly different ways. The thanksgivings are reports about the apostle's own prayers in which he thanked God for the Christians' progress in faith, love, and hope and recalled what God had done and was doing through them. The benedictions declare God to be "blessed," especially for what God has done through Christ. The doxologies praise God as the one who lives forever. These prayer forms have roots in the Old Testament and the Jewish tradition. But they have been transformed through Paul's convictions about God's saving action in and through Christ and given a new context in the paschal mystery. They are now among the most common forms of Christian liturgical prayer.

Paul's reminder in Romans 8:26-27 that God the Father and the Holy Spirit want to help us to pray is a very important contribution to the New Testament teaching about prayer. When we pray, we are not alone and entirely on our own. Rather, we all admit that left to our own devices, we do not know how to pray as we ought. But, as we have seen in earlier chapters, God wants to answer our prayers (Luke 11:1-13 and 18:1-14), and Jesus intercedes for us with his heavenly Father (John 17). Now Paul assures us that the Holy Spirit also intercedes for us with the Father. Often the best prayer involves our letting God take control of our mind and heart, and getting out of the way of God's powerful action within us and through us.

Think, Pray, and Act

Consider how the Pauline thanksgivings, benedictions, and doxologies might enrich your appreciation of Jesus and your own way of praying.

Think

❧ How often do you thank, bless, and praise God in your prayer?

❧ Do you thank God for your family, co-workers, friends, and members of your Christian community?

❧ Do you ever let God and the Holy Spirit take the initiative in your prayer? What happens when you do?

Pray

❧ Spend some time reading slowly and meditatively the benediction in Ephesians 1:3-14, and try to absorb what God has done for us in and through Christ.

❧ Make a prayer of thanksgiving to God for the spiritual progress of the members of your parish and Christian community.

Act

❧ Thank two or three persons in word or writing for their good example in promoting the spread of the gospel and for contributing to the good spirit of the church. Also assure them of your prayers.

Chapter Six

Praises of the Risen Christ in Revelation

Many Catholics are afraid of the Book of Revelation. Those who try to make their way through it find much of it puzzling, especially its exotic imagery and fascination with numbers (the sevens, 666). Many also object to what they perceive as its promotion and even glorification of violence. Moreover, they tend to associate the book with fundamentalist preachers, who interpret it in terms of current events and are invariably proven wrong.

In fact, however, when read in context, Revelation promotes nonviolent resistance on the part of Christians. It is very much the book of the risen Christ, and it looks forward to the full coming of God's kingdom. It is full of hymns and doxologies in praise of God as Creator and Lord and of Christ, the Lamb of God, who fully deserves the title "King of kings and Lord of lords" (Revelation 19:16). Thus Revelation is a fitting conclusion to the New Testament and to the Christian Bible as a whole. But it takes an open mind and a fertile imagination to appreciate it.

A CRISIS AND A RESPONSE

An "apocalypse" is a narrative about a dream or a vision concerning the heavenly world or the future course of history. The term derives from the Greek word *apokalypsis,* which means "revelation." So the last book in the Christian Bible is alternatively called the Book of Revelation or the Apocalypse. The literary form of an apocalypse is found in the Book of Daniel and in the Dead Sea scrolls' *1 Enoch*, as well as two large Jewish works also from the late first century A.D., known as 4 Ezra and 2 Baruch. Each of the three synoptic gospels attributes an apocalyptic discourse to Jesus (Matthew 24–25; Mark 13; Luke 21).

The New Testament Book of Revelation is an apocalypse (1:1) and a prophecy (1:3) in letter form (1:4). It is written in a Semitic Greek style, and its language is generally regarded to be of poor quality. While the writer never quotes an Old Testament text directly, the book is full of biblical allusions and echoes. It features various series of "sevens"—letters (2:1–3:22); seals (6:1–8:1); trumpets (8:7–11:19); bowls (16:1-21); and endtime events (19:11–22:5).

The author of Revelation was a Jewish-Christian prophet named John. He was probably not the apostle or the evangelist. In its various forms, John was a common name among Jews. He was in exile on the island of Patmos (1:9), off the coast of western Asia Minor, for bearing witness to Christ. He claims to have been granted a vision of the risen Christ on "the Lord's day" (1:10) and sought to share it with members of seven Christian communities on the mainland of Asia Minor. The composition of the book is usually placed in A.D. 95–96, the last years in the reign of the emperor Domitian, though it may contain earlier material from Nero's time.

The communities addressed in Revelation were facing, or perhaps already experiencing, persecution for their Christian faith. The persecution seems to have been a limited rather than an empire-wide program that was promoted by a local political official or religious leader. It focused on the Christians' refusal to worship the emperor as a god as well as their refusal to worship the goddess Roma as the personification of the Roman Empire. It was said that the Emperor Domitian liked to be called "my Lord and my God." By promoting these cults of worship, the local officials could presumably win favor with the emperor and his supporters.

In this context, the Christians of western Asia Minor had to confront the question, "Who really is my Lord and my God?" Their response—it is Jesus and his heavenly Father—would make impossible, on the grounds of conscience, their participation in cults worshiping the emperor and the goddess Roma. Revelation's response to this crisis was to use various prayers and hymns that celebrate the risen Christ as Lord and God, on the same level as the one and only God, the Creator and Lord of the universe. These prayer texts were either already in use in the communities being addressed by John or composed by John himself. They play an important role in establishing the divine status of the risen Jesus and in encouraging fearful believers.

The epistolary address in Revelation 1:4-8 contains not only the usual identifications of the author and the recipients ("John to the seven churches that are in Asia") but also a doxology in 1:5-6 that celebrates what God has brought about through Jesus' death and resurrection:

> [5] . . . Jesus Christ, the faithful witness, the firstborn of the dead, and the ruler of the kings of the earth. To him who loves us and freed us from our sins by his blood, [6]and made us to be a kingdom, priests serving his God and Father, to him be glory and dominion forever and ever. Amen. (Revelation 1:5-6)

The doxology formula ("to him be glory and dominion forever and ever. Amen.") is directed to the risen Christ. It celebrates Christ's love for humankind that has been made manifest in his redeeming and liberating death. The expression "freed us from our sins by his blood" interprets Jesus' death on the cross as a sacrifice that has brought about atonement for sins. The description of the new relationship with God made possible through Christ's death ("a kingdom, priests serving his God and Father") draws on terms used in Exodus 19:6 to describe the ancient Israelites gathered with Moses at Mount Sinai: "you shall be for me a priestly kingdom and a holy nation." John's reuse of this biblical terminology attributes to the suffering Christians the dignity promised to God's people at Sinai. So it envisions them as a priesthood charged with caring for the proper worship of God. In the context in which Revelation was composed, the point was that the risen Christ has done what no emperor could ever do. As the faithful witness and the firstborn of the dead, he is the real "ruler of the kings of the earth" (Revelation 1:5) and the "King of kings and Lord of lords" (19:16; see 17:14).

Hymns in the Heavenly Throne Room

In Revelation 4:1 John says that he saw "in heaven a door open," and heard the invitation, "Come up here, and I will show you what must take place after this." As we have seen, an apocalypse is a narrative about a vision or a dream concerning the heavenly world and/or the future course of history. John's report of his experience in Revelation 4–5 describes both what he saw in the heavenly realm and how what he saw set in motion the events associated with the full coming of God's kingdom.

What he saw, according to chapter 4, was a throne and one seated on it (God) bathed in brilliant light and splendor. And around the throne were twenty-four elders and their thrones (twelve times two = symbols of the people of God); the seven spirits of God (the Holy Spirit times seven); and the four living creatures (see Ezekiel 1). Amidst all this spectacle, what he heard first was a song in praise of the one seated on the throne from the four living creatures:

> [8]And the four living creatures, each of them with six wings, are full of eyes all around and inside. Day and night without ceasing they sing,
> "Holy, holy, holy,
> the Lord God the Almighty,
> who was and is and is to come."
> (Revelation 4:8)

Their hymn begins with the triple "holy" found in Isaiah 6:3. Here God is first identified as the "Lord God," which was not only a common biblical way of naming God but also the very titles being applied to the emperor. God is also called "the Almighty" (see also Revelation 11:17; 15:3; 16:7; and 21:22) instead of "the Lord of hosts." Moreover, he is described as the one "who was and who is to come," (see also 1:4; 11:17), a title that seems to be a development from God's self-identification to Moses in Exodus 3:14: "I AM WHO I AM." Note that in their hymn of praise the four living creatures speak the language of the Old Testament Scriptures in order to praise God properly.

They are joined in their hymn of praise by the twenty-four elders, who indicate their subordination to the one seated on the throne by casting their crowns before him. Their hymn takes the form of an acclamation ("You are worthy"), the kind of praise that might be given to a great benefactor or even an emperor. In fact, some scholars think that the scene in Revelation 4 is based on what John and other early Christians might have imagined the imperial throne room to be like.

> [11]"You are worthy, our Lord and God,
>> to receive glory and honor and power,
> for you created all things,
>> and by your will they existed and were created."
> (Revelation 4:11)

What the elders find most worthy of praise in God, who is again called "Lord and God," is his work of creation ("for you created all things"). In the next chapter, the one who is acclaimed to be "worthy" is the risen Jesus, the Lamb of God, on the basis of his work of redemption through his saving death.

As John's vision proceeds in Revelation 5, he sees a scroll written on both sides, with seven seals. This scroll presumably contains a description of what will be the events that make up the future course of history issuing in the fullness of God's kingdom. The problem, as John sees it, is that no one can be found worthy enough to open it and so allow that history to move forward to its final goal.

On being reassured by one the elders that the one who is truly worthy of opening the scroll is "the lion of the tribe of Judah" (see Genesis 49:9) and "the root of David" (see Isaiah 11:1, 10), the risen Christ appears as the "Lamb" who was slain (see Isaiah 53:7). His appearance inspires "a new song" from the four living creatures and the twenty-four elders:

[9] They sing a new song:
  "You are worthy to take the scroll
    and to open its seals,
  for you were slaughtered and by your blood you ran-
      somed for God
    saints from every tribe and language and people and
      nation;
  you have made them to be a kingdom and priests serving
    our God.
(Revelation 5:9-10)

As in Revelation 4:11, the new song takes the form of an acclamation ("You are worthy"). But here the acclamation is directed
to the risen Christ. In fact, all through Revelation, what is said
about God is often also said about the risen Christ. Thus the Book
of Revelation is a powerful witness to the early Christian belief
in the divinity of Jesus. What made the Lamb worthy to open
the seals on the book is the saving significance of his death on
the cross ("by your blood you ransomed for God . . ."). The language applied to the redeemed as "a kingdom and priests" recalls
the doxology in Revelation 1:5-6 and Exodus 19:6.

As the chorus grows in Revelation 5:11, they sing in 5:12
another acclamation to Christ as "the Lamb that was slaughtered" and proclaim that he is "worthy" to receive "power and
wealth and wisdom and might" as gifts or attributes for his own
use and to receive "honor and glory and blessing" from all of
God's creatures. The scene is reminiscent of Daniel's vision of the
heavenly court and the transfer of power from "the Ancient One"
to "one like a son of man" (Daniel 7:13-14). John's vision of the
heavenly court is rounded off with another doxology in Revelation 5:13-14 in which all creation participates:

¹³Then I heard every creature in heaven and on earth and under the earth and in the sea, and all that is in them, singing,

"To the one seated on the throne and to the Lamb
be blessing and honor and glory and might
forever and ever!"

¹⁴And the four living creatures said, "Amen!" And the elders fell down and worshiped.
(Revelation 5:13-14)

HYMNS IN PRAISE OF GOD AND THE LAMB

The acclamation of the risen Jesus (the slain Lamb) as the only one worthy enough to open the seven seals is followed by three series of "sevens": seven seals (Revelation 6:1–8:1); seven trumpets (8:2–11:19); and seven bowls of divine wrath or plagues (15:1–16:21). Interspersed among these septets is the central vision of the defeat of the "unholy trinity." It consists of the beast from the land (the local political or religious leader); the beast from the sea (the Roman emperor); and the great red dragon (Satan) in 12:1–14:20. The book reaches a climax with the vision of the fall of Babylon (= Rome) in 17:1–19:10, a final series of seven eschatological events (19:11–21:8), and the vision of the New Jerusalem (21:9–22:5).

Over the centuries, interpreters of Revelation have argued about the plot or narrative movement of the book. Some view it as a series of repetitions of the same basic dynamic: punishment for the sins of the wicked, rewards for the faithful victorious ones, and the universal recognition of God's sovereignty and justice. This approach views the work as an exercise in recapitulation. Other scholars discern in the apparent repetitions a gradual movement toward a great climax with the appearance of the New Jerusalem near the book's end. There is something to be said for both perspectives. The book is both repetitive in its various scenarios and climactic in the appearance of the New Jerusalem.

In a study of prayers in the New Testament, what is most important is John's use of hymns or hymnlike fragments celebrating the Lord God and the Lamb at key points in the outline. In the interlude between the opening of the sixth and the seventh seals, the "great multitude" issues a word of praise: "Salvation belongs to our God who is seated on the throne, and to the Lamb" (Revelation 7:10). Note that God and the Lamb are treated as equals, thus reinforcing the high Christology that runs through the work. The response of the heavenly court is another doxology celebrating the seven attributes of God being manifested in the display of God's sovereignty and justice:

> 12"Amen! Blessing and glory and wisdom
> and thanksgiving and honor
> and power and might
> be to our God forever and ever! Amen."

(Revelation 7:12)

With the blowing of the seventh trumpet, the heavenly chorus proclaims the victory of our Lord and his Messiah:

> 5And if anyone wants to harm them, fire pours from their mouth and consumes their foes; anyone who wants to harm them must be killed in this manner.

(Revelation 11:5)

In response, the twenty-four elders offer a hymn of thanksgiving:

> [17]"We give you thanks, Lord God Almighty,
>   who are and who were,
> for you have taken your great power
>   and begun to reign.
> [18]The nations raged,
>   but your wrath has come,
>   and the time for judging the dead,
> for rewarding your servants, the prophets
>   and saints and all who fear your name,
>   both small and great,
> and for destroying those who destroy the earth."
> (Revelation 11:17-18)

The thanksgiving addresses God as the "Lord God the Almighty" and as the one who is and was (see Revelation 1:4; 4:8). The future dimension is already being enacted, or is as good as already enacted. The reign of God over all the nations ("the nations raged") is described in terms similar to Psalm 2:1. The reign of God is also described as the time for rewarding the righteous and punishing the wicked.

The central section of Revelation begins in 12:1-9 with the dragon's pursuit of the woman—a symbolic way of depicting Satan's persecution of the church—and the great battle in the heavens where Michael the Archangel casts the dragon/Satan out of heaven. In effect the war against evil has already been won through Jesus' life, death, and resurrection, though the battle on earth goes on. The narrative in Revelation 12 is interrupted by another song from heaven, celebrating the victory of God and his Messiah:

¹⁰Then I heard a loud voice in heaven, proclaiming,
"Now have come the salvation and the power
  and the kingdom of our God
  and the authority of his Messiah,
for the accuser of our comrades has been thrown down,
  who accuses them day and night before our God.
¹¹But they have conquered him by the blood of the Lamb
  and by the word of their testimony,
for they did not cling to life even in the face of death.
¹²Rejoice then, you heavens
  and those who dwell in them!
But woe to the earth and the sea, for the devil has come
    down to you
with great wrath,
  because he knows that his time is short!"
(Revelation 12:10-12)

The "accuser" is an allusion to Satan's former role in Job 1–2, where he convinces God to allow Job to be tested first by loss of his possessions and family, and then by various physical afflictions. While Satan is no longer a member of the heavenly court, he is still active on earth. And in John's view, he is the power behind the persecutions of the church that were being carried out by the two "beasts" in Revelation 13.

The third series of sevens—the bowls of wrath—is introduced by a scene in which the faithful witnesses, who have overcome, sing the "song of Moses" (see Exodus 15:1-18) and the "song of the Lamb." They have conquered the beast (the Roman emperor), its image (a statue of the emperor), and the number 666 signifying the emperor (666 = the numerical value of the name "Nero Caesar"). The reference to the song of Moses prepares for the seven plagues, which are closely tied to the events surrounding ancient Israel's exodus from Egypt.

> [3] And they sing the song of Moses, the servant of God, and the song of the Lamb:
>> "Great and amazing are your deeds,
>>> Lord God the Almighty!
>> Just and true are your ways,
>>> King of the nations!
>> [4] Lord, who will not fear
>>> and glorify your name?
>> For you alone are holy.
>>> All nations will come
>>> and worship before you,
>> for your judgments have been revealed."
>
> (Revelation 15:3-4)

The individual phrases in the song come from various parts of the Old Testament: "great and amazing are your deeds" (see Psalms 111:2; 139:4); "just and true are your ways" (see Psalms 145:17; Deuteronomy 32:4); and so on. The song praises God's works and words. It asks how anyone could fail to fear and glorify God, and looks to all the nations to acknowledge God as the holy one. What is especially celebrated is that God's righteous acts and just judgments have been or soon will be revealed. These just judgments are the events that will lead up to the last judgment.

With the second and third bowls of wrath (Revelation 16:3-4), various bodies of water are turned into blood, just as the Nile River was turned into blood in ancient Israel's exodus from Egypt (see Exodus 7:17-21). The series is interrupted by more hymnic material first from "the angel of the waters" in 16:5b-6:

> [5]And I heard the angel of the waters say,
>   "You are just, O Holy One, who are and were,
>   for you have judged these things;
>   [6]because they shed the blood of saints and prophets,
>   you have given them blood to drink.
>   It is what they deserve!"
> (Revelation 16:5-6)

This hymn celebrates the justice of God, the Holy One, in punishing those who had shed the blood of the "saints" ("holy ones"
= the Christian martyrs) and the prophets (see Matthew 23:37
and Luke 13:34). It is fitting punishment that those who had shed
innocent blood should be forced to drink from rivers and streams
befouled with blood. The angel's interpretation is confirmed by
the altar (Revelation 16:7), which declares that God's judgments
are "true and just."

The transition between the fall of the Roman Empire described
before the fact in Revelation 17–18 and the final series of seven
eschatological events in 19:11–21:8 is supplied by what can be
called a victory liturgy in 19:1-10. The various songs feature the
Hebrew word "Hallelujah" (= "Alleluia," meaning "praise the
Lord"). The "great multitude in heaven" (19:1) consists more
likely of angels than Christian martyrs. Their first song (19:1b-2)
interprets the fall of the Roman Empire as proof of God's justice
and as punishment for putting God's servants to death:

> [1]After this I heard what seemed to be the loud voice of a
> great multitude in heaven, saying,
>   "Hallelujah!

Salvation and glory and power to our God,
   [2]for his judgments are true and just;
he has judged the great whore
   who corrupted the earth with her fornication,
and he has avenged on her the blood of his servants."
(Revelation 19:1-2)

Their second song (Revelation 19:3) stresses the definitive character of Rome's defeat: "Hallelujah. The smoke goes up from her forever and ever." The members of the inner circle of the heavenly court—the twenty-four elders and the four living creatures—affirm the angelic song by saying, "Amen. Hallelujah" (19:4), which means "I believe it so. Praise the Lord." The voice coming from the throne is most likely one of the elders or living creatures, and it too is a call for all to praise God. The final song (19:6-8) is from the entire heavenly chorus:

[6]Then I heard what seemed to be the voice of a great multitude, like the sound of many waters and like the sound of mighty thunderpeals, crying out,
  "Hallelujah!
  For the Lord our God
    the Almighty reigns.
  [7]Let us rejoice and exult
    and give him the glory,
  for the marriage of the Lamb has come,
    and his bride has made herself ready;
  [8]to her it has been granted to be clothed
    with fine linen, bright and pure"—
  for the fine linen is the righteous deeds of the saints.
(Revelation 19:6-8)

It first celebrates the establishment of God's reign in its fullness. Then in Revelation 19:7b-8 it describes this event as the wedding feast of the Lamb. The image is based on various Old Testament passages (see Hosea 2:16-22; Isaiah 54:5-6; 62:5; Ezekiel 16:6-14) that portray God's relationship with Israel in terms of a marriage. Thus in turn, idolatry is described as fornication or prostitution (see Hosea 2:4-15; Ezekiel 16:15-63). Here the bride of the Lamb is the people of God, which in Revelation is the church. In contrast to ancient Israel, which according to the prophets fell repeatedly into idolatry, the church is a faithful bride. In contrast to the prostitute Roma who dresses garishly like a prostitute (see Revelation 17:1-6), the church-bride wears "fine linen, bright and pure," which is symbolic of moral purity and her fidelity in facing martyrdom. An interchange between the angelic interpreter and John rounds off the passage in 19:9-10.

"Come, Lord Jesus"

The final verses in Revelation (22:6-21) appear to be a collection of disparate sayings, much like the end of the book of Daniel (12:4-13). The ten sayings revolve around three major themes: the authenticity of the prophet's message, the imminence of the Lord's coming ("I am coming soon"), and exhortations to remain faithful. Since these are major themes in the book, the ten sayings constitute a fitting summary or epilogue.

The tenth and final saying (Revelation 22:20b-21) has two parts. The first part (22:20b) is a prayer expressing the hope that the risen Christ will return soon: "Amen. Come, Lord Jesus!" It is the Greek form of the same prayer quoted in its original Aramaic wording in 1 Corinthians 16:22: "Maranatha." In Aramaic the term for "our Lord" is *maran* or *marana*, depending on the dialect, and the singular imperative for "come" is *atha* or *tha*, depending on the dialect. The fact that Paul quoted it in Aramaic suggests that it was a very early Christian prayer, going back to the Palestinian Jewish Christian community. The prayer is an appropriate way to close the Book of Revelation, since the second coming of Jesus will be the pivotal factor in the full coming of God's kingdom.

The second part (Revelation 22:21) of the final saying is a wish that is at the same time a prayer: "the grace of the Lord Jesus be with all the saints. Amen." Similar blessings appear at the end of many other New Testament epistles (1 Corinthians 16:23; 2 Corinthians 13:13; and so on). Whether it was written by John or added later by a scribe, it provides a nice complement to the prayer for Jesus' second coming in 22:20b. It asks God in the time between the first and second comings of Jesus for the divine favor or "grace" to sustain us and give us peace so that we might live in faith, love, and hope. Taken together, these two prayers are a fitting conclusion to the Christian Bible, since as Christians we walk between the times of Jesus' first and second comings.

Bringing the Contexts Together

Those who have worked through this book will recognize that the Revelation is not as strange as it may once have seemed. The language of the book is thoroughly biblical. Even though John never speaks explicitly about Scripture being fulfilled, almost every verse contains an allusion to or an echo of the Old Testament. Nevertheless, the theological context—the saving significance of Jesus' life, death, and resurrection, and hope for his second coming—places the Old Testament in a decidedly new context. And as we have seen throughout this book, context is everything, or at least almost everything.

The basic theology of Revelation is not far from that of the Lord's Prayer (Matthew 6:9-13 and Luke 11:2-4). John tries to envision and depict what he imagines the full coming of God's kingdom will be like—when all creation "hallows" the name of God, and God's will is done on earth as it is in heaven. He also tries to describe what all this might mean for the faithful remnant. While they can and should look forward to eternal life with God, they will nevertheless undergo trials and tribulations. Therefore, as they wait patiently and nonviolently, they will need physical and spiritual sustenance or "daily bread," forgiveness of sins or "trespasses," and deliverance from evil or "the evil one."

The Book of Revelation has exercised enormous influence on Christian music. It has been the inspiration for such popular hymns as "Holy God, We Praise Thy Name," "The Battle Hymn of the Republic," "We Shall Overcome," and many other popular Christian hymns. The famous "Hallelujah Chorus" in Handel's *Messiah* ("King of kings and Lord of lords") is right out of the Book of Revelation. The hymnic pieces scattered throughout the book illustrate the power of song in prayer. As we have seen, whenever John wishes to highlight a moment or event in one of his apocalyptic scenarios, he inserts a hymnic piece. So great is his faith and joy that he can only express them adequately through songs. Thus he confirms the principle that those who sing pray twice.

There is no need to fear the Book of Revelation. Read it in its biblical context and its historical and literary contexts with the Lord's Prayer as your guide, and enter into its hymns in praise of the one who truly is "King of kings and Lord of lords." Make its praises your own.

Think, Pray, and Act

Consider how the hymns of praise in Revelation might enrich your appreciation of Jesus and your own way of praying.

Think

♪ How do the hymnic parts of Revelation portray Jesus in relation to God the Father?

♪ Does reading Revelation in light of the Lord's Prayer help you understand the book better?

♪ What might it mean today to proclaim the risen Jesus as "King of kings and Lord of lords"?

Pray

♪ Imagine yourself alongside John the Seer in the heavenly court in Revelation 4–5. What do you see? What do you hear? How might you respond?

♪ Imagine yourself as part of the "victory liturgy" in Revelation 19:1-10. What do you see? What do you hear? How might you respond?

Act

♪ Some hymnbooks note the biblical origin of the words in their songs. If you have access to such a hymnal, look for hymns inspired especially by the Book of Revelation.

For Further Study

Charlesworth, James H. ed. *The Lord's Prayer and Other Prayer Texts from the Greco-Roman Era*. Valley Forge, PA: Trinity Press International, 1994.

Cullmann, Oscar. *Prayer in the New Testament*. Minneapolis: Fortress, 1995.

Farris, Stephen. *The Hymns of Luke's Infancy Narratives. Their Origin, Meaning, and Significance*. Sheffield, UK: JSOT Press, 1985.

Heinemann, Joseph. *Prayer in the Talmud: Forms and Patterns*. Berlin-New York: de Gruyter, 1977.

Heinemann, Joseph with Jakob J. Petuchowski. *Literature of the Synagogue*. Piscataway, NJ: Gorgias, 2006.

Karris, Robert J. *Prayer and the New Testament*. New York: Crossroad, 2000.

Karris, Robert J. *A Symphony of New Testament Hymns*. Collegeville: Liturgical Press, 1996.

Kiley, Mark et al. eds. *Prayer from Alexander to Constantine: A Critical Anthology*. New York: Routledge, 1997.

Longenecker, Richard N. ed. *Into God's Presence: Prayer in the New Testament*. Grand Rapids: Eerdmans, 2001.

Neyrey, Jerome H. *Give God the Glory: Ancient Prayer and Worship in Cultural Perspective.* Grand Rapids: Eerdmans, 2007.

Wiles, Gordon P. *Paul's Intercessory Prayers: The Significance of Intercessory Passages in Paul's Letters.* Cambridge: Cambridge University Press, 1974.

Wright, N. T. *The Lord and His Prayer.* Grand Rapids: Eerdmans, 1997.

the WORD
among us ®
The *Spirit* of Catholic Living

T his book was published by The Word Among Us. For nearly thirty years, The Word Among Us has been answering the call of the Second Vatican Council to help Catholic laypeople encounter Christ in the Scriptures—a call reiterated recently by Pope Benedict XVI and a Synod of Bishops.

The name of our company comes from the prologue to the Gospel of John and reflects the vision and purpose of all of our publications: to be an instrument of the Spirit, whose desire is to manifest Jesus' presence in and to the children of God. In this way, we hope to contribute to the church's ongoing mission of proclaiming the gospel to the world and growing ever more deeply in our love for the Lord.

Our monthly devotional magazine, *The Word Among Us*, features meditations on the daily and Sunday Mass readings, and currently reaches more than one million Catholics in North America each year and another 500,000 Catholics in 100 countries. Our press division has published nearly 180 books and Bible studies over the past ten years.

To learn more about who we are and what we publish, log on to our Web site at **www.wau.org**. There you will find a variety of Catholic resources that will help you grow in your faith.

Embrace His Word, Listen to God . . .